LET'S GO SAILING

by Peter Isler

Foreword by Dennis Conner

Illustrations and Design by
Vince Mattera

Photography by Lenny Shabes

Acknowledgements

There are many people who contributed to this book. I would like to thank the entire staff of the American Sailing Association for their help and support. Scott Stokes did a superb job as editor of the book as did Cynthia Shabes and Martin McCarthy with the copy editing. Vince Mattera and typesetter Leslie Luoma were a pleasure to work with. Lenny Shabes, along with taking the photographs, was especially inspirational. Many thanks to Captain Hal Sutphen, USN Director of Navy Sailing, for his excellent technical review. My appreciation also goes to Jim Stewart at Hobie Cat for the loan of the boats for the photographs and to California Pacific in Mission Bay, CA. for their co-operation. Also providing boats and sailing gear was Action Sailing Center in Marina del Rey, CA. Amy Wardell, who is shown in many pictures, was an especially helpful "model" and good natured subject for the repeated capsize photos! My wife, JJ, helped me throughout the writing of this book and provided expert guidance in keeping me focused on the important points. Finally, I would like to thank all of the people, sailing instructors, and sailors who have helped me learn more and more about this wonderful sport. Special thanks to Pelham Grey for his support and help.

ASA Directors

Steven Fargnoli	Seth Rosner
Daniel Fioroni	Lenny Shabes
Reed Freyermuth	Peter Sprague
Peter Isler	Kit Watson
Harlan Lee	Chuck Wilk

ASA Advisors

Robert Black	Gary Jobson
Briggs Dalzell	Robert Johnstone
Cy Gillette	Bruce Kirby
Pelham Grey	Barry Labow
Stan Honey	Lowell North
Gary Hoyt	Paul Miller
J.J. Isler	Jack Sommer

DUE TO ONGOING CHANGES IN GOVERNMENTAL SAFETY AND NAVIGATION REGULATIONS, THE PRUDENT SAILOR SHOULD KEEP ABREAST OF ANY SUCH CHANGES SINCE THE DATE OF THIS PUBLICATION BY CONTACTING THE NEAREST U.S. COAST GUARD REPRESENTATIVE.

A FIRESIDE BOOK
PUBLISHED BY THE AMERICAN SAILING ASSOCIATION
AND SIMON & SCHUSTER, INC.

Copyright© 1987 by the American Sailing Association

All rights reserved **ISBN 0-671-65923-5**

No part of this book may be reproduced in any form without written permission from the American Sailing Association

Printed in the United States of America

Published by the American Sailing Association
13922 Marquesas Way
Marina Del Rey, CA 90292

Table of Contents

You and the American Sailing Association

Lenny Shabes - ASA President

"Let's Go Sailing" is written in conjunction with the American Sailing Association (ASA)—America's Sail Education Authority. The ASA is a group of sailors who are dedicated to boating safety through education. At the heart of these collective efforts is a comprehensive educational system based on internationally recognized Standards. The ASA system has been designed to serve as a guide while you experience the fun and excitement of sailing. This book is just your first step.

Most likely you have chosen to learn sailing through an organized program at a yacht club, camp, community boating program or sailing school. That's good. You are about to benefit from a proven structured system which helps you learn more and progress faster.

A key element of this system is the *Sailing Log Book*. The *Log Book* has been designed to serve as a personal record of your sailing experience and outlines the International Standards of sailing proficiency. This record will be especially useful in documenting your knowledge and experience for the prestigious *Presidential Sports Award for Sailing*. More information about obtaining your copy of the *Sailing Log Book* can be found on the inside back cover of this book.

You are strongly encouraged to seize the spirit of national and self pride by documenting your time in the sport and achieving the *Presidential Sailing Award*. The ASA, in cooperation with the President's Council on Physical Fitness and the Amateur Athletic Union, is proud to help you prepare for your sailing achievements now and in the future.

Foreword

by Dennis Conner

You are taking the first step into a sport that can give you a lifetime of enjoyment and challenge. I spend most of my days on the water locked in competition. For me sailboat racing is fun, especially when you are winning the *America's Cup!* But racing is not for everyone and that is the beauty about sailing—there are so many ways to enjoy it.

Like you, I started sailing on a small, centerboard boat in San Diego when I was a kid. Starting off by learning in a small boat is the right way. You are going to find out very soon, just like all of us sailors, how much fun this sport really is. Take your time to enjoy your first lessons on the water because having fun is really the bottom line.

One of the best things that happened from all of the publicity surrounding the *America's Cup* is that millions of Americans were introduced to sailing for the very first time. You don't need a 12 Meter like *STARS and STRIPES* to go sailing. You can have just as much fun on a 12 foot dinghy. Sailing is easy to learn and will give you pleasure for the rest of your life.

I have known Peter Isler as a sailor and teacher for many years now. Besides helping me win the 1987 *America's Cup* as my navigator, he is also deeply involved in helping people of all ages get started in our great sport. That is one of the reasons Peter helped found the *American Sailing Association*. This book, *"LET'S GO SAILING,"* is a perfect starting point for you. With his fresh, concise approach, Peter has made it easy for you to get going in sailing by helping you develop proper skills and build your confidence. Read this book, learn from it and get ready for a whole new world out on the water. Who knows where it may take you!

Introduction:

There is really nothing like sailing. It's an activity that can take you across the harbor or around the world. There is so much here for you—a sport that is part science and part art. You can find peace and relaxation aboard a sailboat or a world of challenges.

Welcome to the rich and wonderful world of sailing. There is enough here to keep us all learning more for the rest of our lives. And it's easy to get started. With the proper instruction, soon you will be enjoying this wonderful sport. I have written this book to help you get the most out of your introduction to sailing. I have gotten so much enjoyment, traveled all around the world and met thousands of interesting people, thanks to my involvement in the sport. You don't have to be an international calibre racer to enjoy sailing. In fact, some of my best memories are when everything was new and fresh; when I was learning how to sail. I have tried to bring myself back to that time to make this book as valuable as possible for you, the new sailor. I have tried to point out the common pitfalls as I see them, such as overdoing the new vocabulary of sailing, and I have tried to focus on the important stuff such as wind direction and keeping the boat moving. Hopefully, you will get as much enjoyment out of sailing as I have. This book is intended to help make your first few steps in the world of sailing a little easier. So let's go. There is a new world awaiting you.

Peter Isler

This book is an introduction to small boat sailing. In my opinion, you have chosen the best type of boat on which to learn. You can learn to sail on any sailboat. But centerboard (and daggerboard) boats are more responsive than their larger, heavier cousins—the keel boats. Therefore, the effects of the wind, sail trim, crewing and steering are easy to see and learn on a centerboard boat. Whether your goal is to sail small boats in your local waters or cruise around the world, your introduction to sailing in a centerboard boat will serve you well.

Beginning to Sail

A Sailor's Important Relationship with the Wind

If you have ever spent any time on or near the water, you have experienced a whole new world. Winds can whip up the water's surface into foamy waves in no time. Or lack of wind can leave the surface as smooth as glass. Out on the water in a sailboat your interest in wind and weather grows. Your ability to *accurately sense changes in the wind, its speed and its direction* will improve as you learn to sail. This is an important change that will occur as you become a sailor.

By feeling the wind on your face you can tell its direction.

Because your boat is so dependent on the wind, your ability to assess its direction and speed is important. In fact, the first step in learning to sail is to increase your sensitivity and awareness of the wind. I wish my first sailing instructor had impressed this point upon me. The most direct way to track the wind is simply to **feel it**. Your body, especially your exposed face, can feel the exact direction of the wind if you concentrate. Practice "feeling" the wind whenever you can. There is probably *no more important first step in learning to sail*.

Visual aids can be used to determine the wind direction. By looking at the water we can see waves or maybe tiny ripples.

This *water motion is caused by the wind* and you can determine the wind direction by looking at the ripples which are generated at 90 degrees to the wind. Once you gain more experience, you will be able to assess the wind speed by looking at the water. For example, white caps begin to form on waves at 12 knots of wind speed. Strong water flow or current can also create waves.

Other visual signs include *anchored boats* which will point into the wind unless there is a strong current. A *flag* or *wind vane* on the top of a mast can show the wind; so can a *flapping sail* which will wave in the wind like a flag. On your own boat short pieces of yarn or cassette tape tied to the wire rigging can provide that critical wind information.

The bottom line is that *assessing the wind's direction is of utmost importance to sailors*. When you are just starting out you may feel as I did, so inundated with this new world of sheets and sails and bows and reaches, that it is easy to lose track of the all important wind direction. If this happens, relax, and just **feel the wind on your face** because a sailor's world revolves around the wind and you are going to become a sailor. In this book I will try to keep extraneous information to a minimum. Sure, in time you will learn a lot more than you do in your first few sails. But you have plenty of time and your goal is to learn to sail first.

The Sailor's Language

Your next step is to feel comfortable and at home on your sailboat. As anyone who has read Mutiny on the Bounty or Moby Dick knows, sailing has its own language—terminology that makes it easier to sail a boat. It will take some time before you are comfortable with all of these new terms. *Don't force it or get too involved in learning every little name for every little piece on the boat right away.* You want to sail the boat, not talk about it. With time and practice you will assimilate this new language and it will become your own.

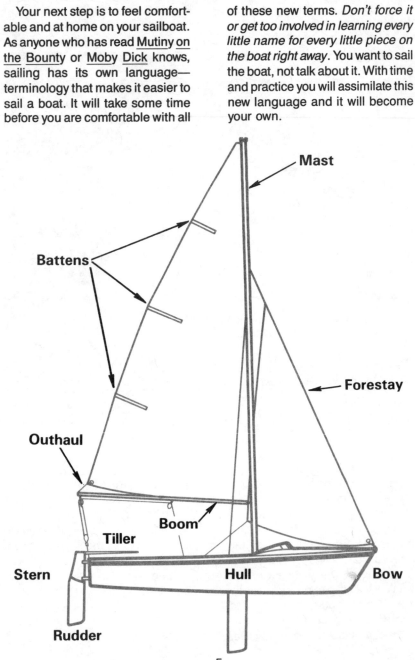

We will now introduce the major words for parts of the boat and sailing terms that you will be exposed to on your first sail. They will become old friends soon, so just review them every so often until you are comfortable with them. You should know that every sailboat is slightly different in the way it is constructed and designed. You may find that the boat you are learning to sail on has its own special systems or parts that will vary from the generic boat we are using.

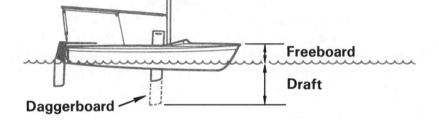

Freeboard

Draft

Daggerboard

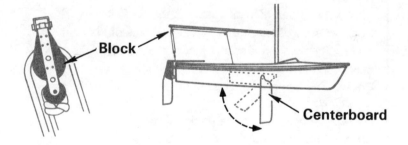

Block

Centerboard

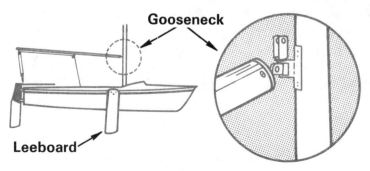

Gooseneck

Leeboard

PARTS OF A BOAT

Hull: The body of the boat

Bow: The front end

Forward: Direction towards the bow

Stern: The back end

Aft: Direction towards the stern

Waterline Length: Length of the boat in the water

Beam: Sailboat's maximum width

Freeboard: Height of the hull above the water

Draft: Distance from the water's surface to the bottom of the boat

Cockpit: Inside of the boat where the crew sits

Centerboard: A pivoting fin that can project down into the water to counteract the force of the sails, preventing side slip

Centerboard Trunk: Housing for the centerboard

Daggerboard: Same as a centerboard except it slides up and down a vertical slot instead of pivoting.

Leeboard: Similar to a centerboard, mounted on the side of the hull

Thwart: A structural cross beam in the cockpit

Rudder: A movable steering fin at the back of the boat

Tiller: The steering arm that moves the rudder

Mast: The vertical main pole supporting the sails

Boom: The hinged, horizontal pole supporting the bottom of the mainsail

Forestay: Forward wire supporting the mast

Shrouds (or side-stays): Side wires supporting the mast

Standing Rigging: Forestay, shrouds, backstay

Mast Step: Fitting in boat upon which mast stands

Gooseneck: Hinged attachment point for the boom on the mast

Chain Plate: Attachment point for shrouds and headstay on hull

Hiking Straps: Foot straps used to lean out (hike out) over the side of the boat

Buoyancy Tanks: Airtight compartments that provide flotation in the event of a capsize

Hiking Stick: A tiller attachment allowing for easier steering from a variety of seating positions

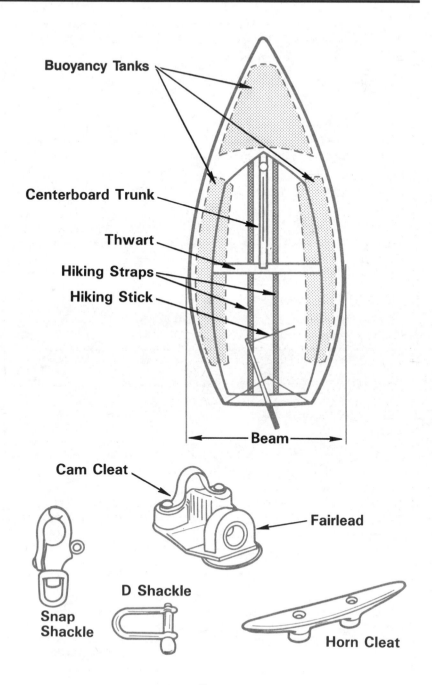

Buoyancy Tanks

Centerboard Trunk

Thwart

Hiking Straps

Hiking Stick

Beam

Cam Cleat

Fairlead

Snap Shackle

D Shackle

Horn Cleat

Jib: Front sail hoisted on the forestay

Main: Primary sail set on the mast and boom

Genoa: A large jib that overlaps the mast

Spinnaker: A balloonlike sail used for downwind sailing

Head: Top of sail

Tack: Front lower corner of sail

Clew: Back lower corner of sail

Luff: Front edge of sail

Leech: Back edge of sail

Foot: Bottom edge of sail

Battens: Wood or fiberglass slats inserted into pockets on the sail's back side (leech) to help control sail shape

Sheets: Ropes used to control the adjustment or trim of a sail (eg., mainsheet, jibsheet)

Halyards: Rope or wire used to hoist sails on masts or on wire stays

Lines: Another name for rope

Cleats: Fittings of various designs used to secure ropes

Blocks: Rope or wire pulley

Traveler: Adjustable system upon which the mainsheet block(s) can slide

Fairlead: A block or eye used as a guide to fix the point of trim for a jibsheet

Running Rigging: Movable rigging, including sheets, blocks, halyards, lines, etc.

Outhaul: Adjustable system at back end of boom securing the mainsail clew. Used to adjust the tension on the foot of the sail

Downhaul or Cunningham: Rope or mechanical system near the gooseneck used to adjust the tension of the front edge (luff) of the mainsail

Shackle: U-shaped metal device used to fasten sails and fittings

Boom Vang: Rigging from the boom to the bottom of the mast that stops boom from lifting when reaching and running

There, that's not so bad. Remember, it will take you some time to master this terminology. But as you spend time on the boat these terms will become very familiar. So let's leave these terms to review later and get on to what we are really here for—**sailing**. If you forget an item's name while you are sailing, don't worry about it. You will have plenty of time to learn these new names.

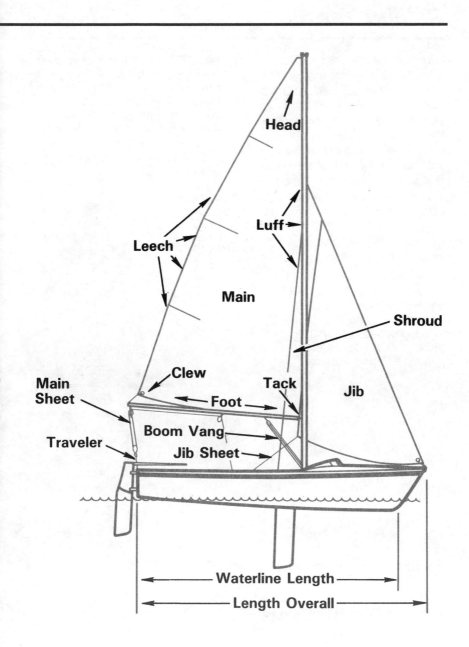

Head

Luff

Leech

Main

Shroud

Clew

Main
Sheet

Tack

Jib

Foot

Traveler

Boom Vang

Jib Sheet

Waterline Length

Length Overall

Sailing Terms

Let's go back to the basics—*the boat, the sails and the wind*. In case you did not know, a sailboat cannot sail directly towards the wind. But by using the lifting forces created by air and water flow over the wing-shaped sails and centerboard, a sailboat can sail remarkably close to the wind. On average, a modern sailboat can sail within about 45 degrees of the wind direction. This is a big improvement over the square riggers which had a hard time sailing any closer than 90 degrees to the wind.

It is not necessary to understand how a sailboat can sail "upwind" (45 degrees to the wind) to be able to get out there and do it. If you want to learn more about the physics of sailing, take a trip to the library. For the most scientifically inclined there are two books by C.A. Marchaj that explore the subjects of the aerodynamics and hydrodynamics of sailing in great depth.

So *let's start with the wind direction to orient ourselves* and learn the **points of sail.**

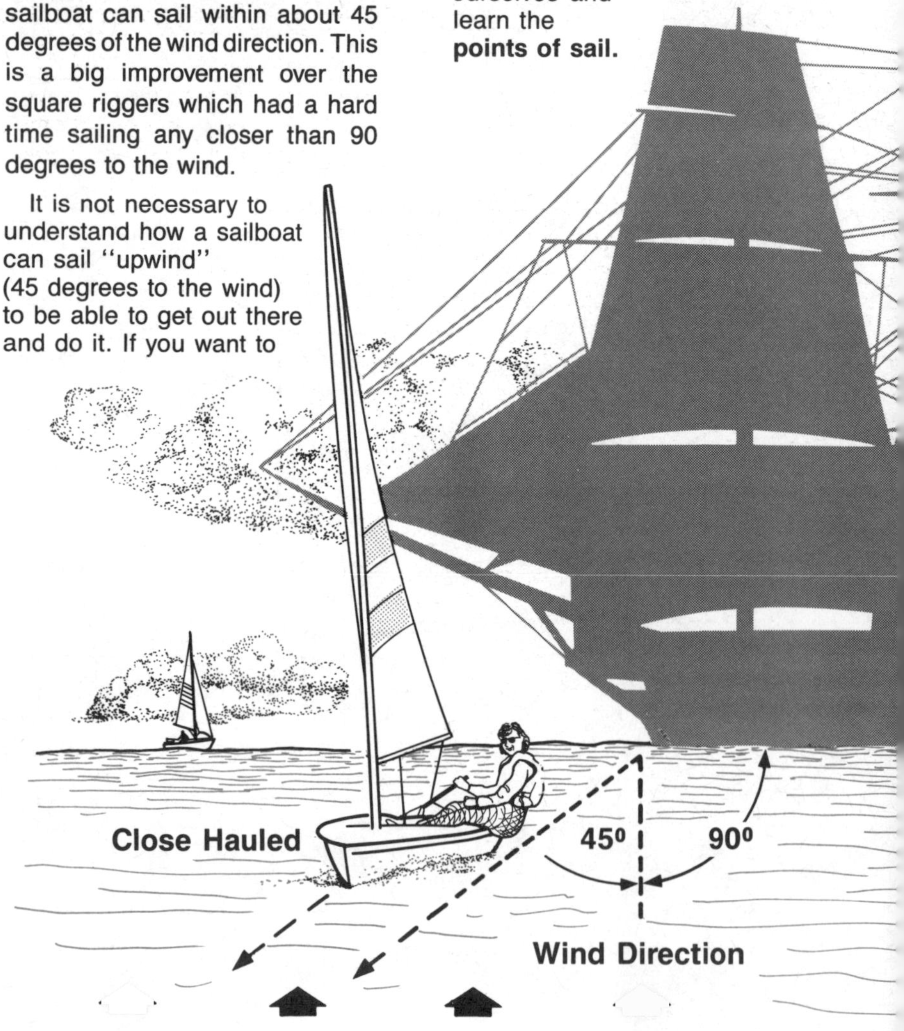

Close Hauled

45°   90°

Wind Direction

11

Close Hauled: Sailing "upwind" as close as possible to the wind (about 45 degrees)

Reaching: A reach is any point of sail between closehauled and running.

Reaching can be divided into three finer points of sail:

Close reach: Closer than 90 degrees to the wind

Beam reach: Sailing 90 degrees to the wind

Broad reach: Between beam reaching and running

Running: Sailing directly downwind with the wind coming from straight behind

Running

Reaching

Wind Direction

Points of Sail

On paper (depicted by a diagram), the points of sail are easy to see. The challenge is to apply this diagram to the real world on the boat. This is when your ability to *feel the wind* will be very valuable. As you can see, there is really only a 90 degree sector bisected by the wind direction where you cannot sail a boat (no sail zone). Traveling in any other direction is possible and really quite easy. The main key remains to be *aware* of the wind direction.

The easiest way I know to remember **port** and **starboard** is that the word "left" has fewer letters than "right" and so does its nautical term "port" compared to "starboard". To be honest, I have slipped back to using the words right and left on a boat. There is certainly no magic in their nautical counterparts.

Port: left side (facing towards bow)

Starboard: right side

However, there is one time when the nautical right and left come in handy. That's when we are describing *upon which side of the boat the wind is blowing.*

Port   Starboard

This boat is sailing on port tack with the wind blowing over the left side of the boat.

13

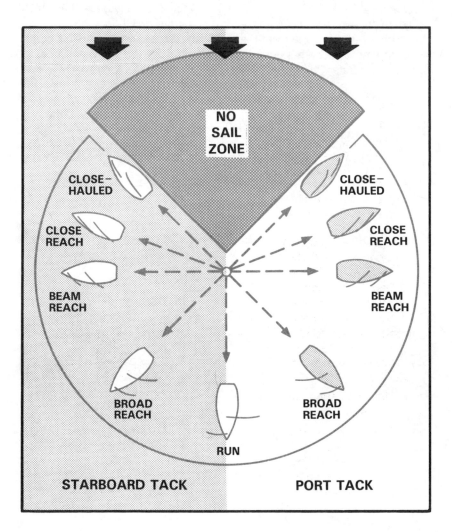

As you can see from the diagram, a **beam reach** can be accomplished with the wind hitting either the right or the left side. To differentiate we introduce the terms **starboard** and **port tack**. There are a couple of tricks to determining what tack your boat is on. First is, you guessed it, by simply *feeling* the wind direction. If it is coming over the left side your boat is sailing along the port tack. Another aid is to *see* upon what side of the boat the sails are set. If the wind is blowing the mainsail and boom out over the right side of the boat, then you are sailing on port tack. Starboard tack has the opposite features.

How Sails Work

There are two ways a sail works. Like the wing of a plane (with the wind flowing over both sides), or like a parachute ("blocking" the wind). When you are sailing upwind, close-hauled or beam reaching, the wind flows across both sides of the wing shape of the sails creating lift and forward motion. This, combined with the force of the water flowing across the centerboard, allows the boat to go forward and want to heel over. This combination of wind and water pressure drives the boat forward. On a broad reach or a run there is very little flow across the sails, which are now acting like a parachute, and the wind merely pushes the sails forward which in turn push the boat forward.

Running

Broad Reaching

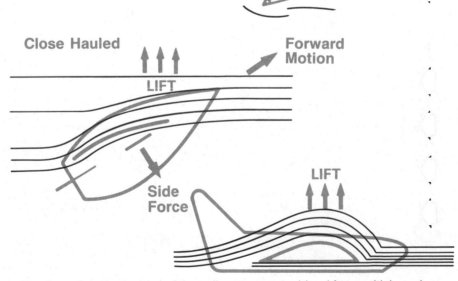

Close Hauled

Forward Motion

LIFT

Side Force

LIFT

The flow along both sides of the sail causes a combined force which pushes the boat at right angles to the boom. Due to the centerboard acting to resist sideslipping in the water, the boat is forced to go forward.

Tacking vs Jibing

Now let's move from the static points of sail to terms that describe *turning* the boat . To change the boat's heading from starboard to port tack or vice versa we can turn the bow of the boat *towards* the wind and through the **zone of no sailing**. This is called **"coming about"** or **"tacking"**. The ultimate result of this maneuver is that the wind blows upon the opposite side of the boat, ie., we have changed tacks.

Another way of *changing tacks* is by **jibing**. To jibe we turn the bow of the boat *away* from the wind until we are past a downwind course. As in the maneuver of coming about the *ultimate result is that the wind blows on the opposite side*. When changing tacks by coming about or jibing, the sails will also change sides as the wind shifts and pushes on them from a different angle. This brings up one of the key distinctions between coming about and jibing.

When coming about the sails will flutter rapidly as the boat is turned through the "no sail zone". *When jibing the sails will remain full of air with no flapping*; but they still change sides and they do it with a vengeance. During a jibe the boom will come flying across with all the force of the wind. After a few friendly reminders from the boom you will learn to keep your head low during this maneuver.

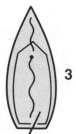

Coming about from port tack to starboard tack.

At stage 2 the tack is begun by gently pushing the tiller away.

The boat will turn into the wind (stage 3).

The crew will change sides now as the boat continues to turn until the sails have filled on the new tack (stage 5).

You must practice this maneuver to get comfortable with how fast to turn the boat.

16

Heading Up, Heading Down

"HEADING UP"

- **Boat turns toward the wind**
- **Sails are trimmed in**

"HEADING DOWN"

- **Boat turns away from wind**
- **Sails are eased out**

Finally, let's learn two words to describe more *subtle turns that do not result in changing tacks* but can change the wind's angle to the boat (**point of sail**). When you turn the boat toward the wind you are **"heading up"**. When you first get your hand on the tiller of a sailboat you may find that it's not quite like steering a car since the boat turns in the opposite direction that you move the tiller. In no time, tiller steering will become second nature. It may be helpful to remember that

to head up you push the tiller toward the side of the boat to which the sails and boom are being blown.

"Heading down" is the opposite of "heading up" and describes any turn of the boat away from the wind direction. You may hear other words or phrases such as "bearing off" or "bear away", but you'll find it simple and easy to use head **up** and head **down**. As long as you keep tabs on the wind direction, the rest will come easily. Practice *feeling* the wind whenever you can. When you

17

get aboard your boat take a look around to learn from which direction the wind is blowing. You will develop your own little tricks for staying on top of the wind direction which, as all sailors learn, never remains 100 percent constant.

When I learned to sail, I would often get my boat stuck dead in the water with no maneuverability. Just like a car, if *your boat isn't moving* *then the steering wheel (tiller) will not have any effect*. I think my main problem was that I was *too concerned with learning all the terms and I did not concentrate on staying tuned to the wind direction*. When the boat is allowed to lose all speed while pointing towards the wind in the **"no sail zone"**, you are said to be "in irons".

- *This boat is "stuck" pointed towards the wind.*

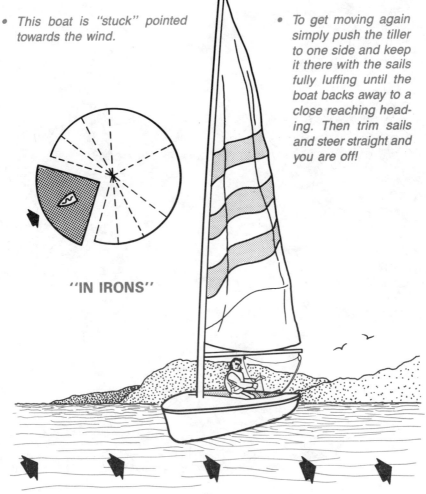

"IN IRONS"

- *To get moving again simply push the tiller to one side and keep it there with the sails fully luffing until the boat backs away to a close reaching heading. Then trim sails and steer straight and you are off!*

Fortunately, it is a lot easier to get out of irons in a centerboard boat than it was for the old square rigged fighting ships who became dead meat for their opponents. All you have to do is keep the tiller turned hard in one steady direction and release the sheets. Soon the boat will back up and turn onto a reach at which time you can trim in and get going.

Another heading to avoid on a sailboat is that which is known as being **"by the lee"**. It occurs when you are sailing downwind with the wind right behind you. If you change course slightly or the wind shifts you can find the wind blowing over the *same side of the boat as the boom*. This is the exact same maneuver as jibing, except it is done unintentionally so that the

boom has not yet changed sides. This is dangerous, since the boom can come charging uncontrollably across the cockpit.

Well, enough of words and concepts. Let's get to the fun by rigging our boat and going for a sail. I hope that I have emphasized the importance of keeping things in perspective. Don't get bogged down with the terminology. Simply *find that* *wind direction and stay attuned to* *it.* The rest will come with time.

Sail Care and Folding

Proper sail care will ensure long life of your sails. Never stuff a sail in a bag. Always make sure a sail is dry if it is going to be left in the bag for over a couple of days. Using two people, fold the sail along the bottom edge (foot) making sure not to crease any plastic windows. Always remove the battens when folding unless they are permanently sewn in the sail.

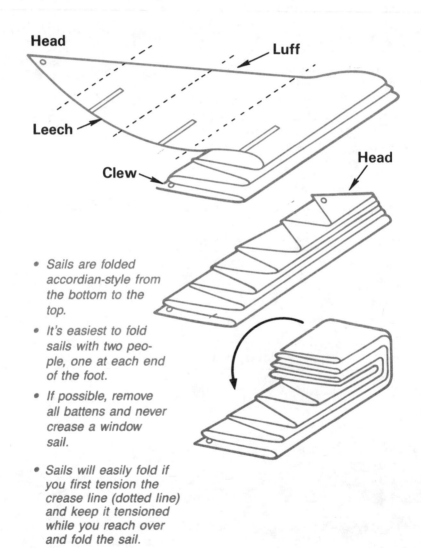

- Sails are folded accordian-style from the bottom to the top.

- It's easiest to fold sails with two people, one at each end of the foot.

- If possible, remove all battens and never crease a window sail.

- Sails will easily fold if you first tension the crease line (dotted line) and keep it tensioned while you reach over and fold the sail.

Review Questions

1. What is the single most important concept for a new sailor to understand?
a) Sailboats work like airplanes
b) A centerboard boat is the best boat on which to learn
c) Port and Starboard
d) The relationship between the boat and the wind
e) Sailing is different on square riggers

2. Which of the following signs help a sailor to determine the wind direction? (May be more than one answer)
a) The direction of the ripples on the water
b) The direction of the current
c) The direction of other sailboats sailing
d) The direction an anchored boat points
e) The feel of the wind on the cheek

3. Why is it important to distinguish between port and starboard tack? (Choose the BEST answer)
a) Because it helps us to understand the points of sail and the concept of changing tacks (tacking or jibing)
b) Because sailboats cannot sail directly upwind
c) Because port is left and starboard is right on a sailboat
d) Because the skipper must be able to feel the wind
e) Because we want to stay out of irons

4. What is the difference between tacking and jibing? (Choose the one BEST answer)
a) One is done on port tack and the other on starboard tack
b) The crew sits on the opposite side of the boat from the skipper
c) One can be done without changing tacks
d) One is changing tacks by turning towards the wind and the other is changing tacks by turning away from the wind
e) Tacking can be done only on centerboard boats

5. How can you avoid being caught "in irons"? (Choose the one BEST answer)
a) Always sail on port tack
b) Always keep the boat moving no matter where you are headed
c) Duck your head when you jibe to avoid being hit with the boom
d) Hoist your main halyard very high
e) Don't sail in tidal waters

Let's Go Sailing

Rigging

It's hard to get too specific with details about rigging. There are so many types of boats, each with its own rigging variations. Your instructor will be the best source of information if you run into any rigging questions. It is also helpful to watch other people rigging their boats at your launching area.

But there are certain common features and rules pertaining to the rigging and launching of sailboats that you can follow. The first step is making sure you have all of the gear and equipment necessary to go sailing. You may laugh, but many a sail has been thwarted because of a forgotten item. It may help to have a *checklist* to ensure that your trip to the water is not wasted.

Much time can be saved if the boat can be stored with the mast up and the sails stowed in the boat. A boat cover will keep everything dry and less prone to theft. Remember the following rule which will come

Before sailing check that all rigging is in proper working order.

23

2

It is important to bend your legs and keep your back vertical when lifting your boat. Always ask for plenty of help. It is a good way to make new friends.

in handy when you own a boat of your own. **THE EASIER IT IS TO GET THE BOAT SAILING, THE MORE SAILING YOU WILL DO.**

However, security or a given storage situation may dictate that you spend some time rigging the boat. Turn this process into a system so that you can do it easily and quickly. The first step is to prepare the boat for launching by setting up the mast if it is not already up.

If the mast is heavy, use two people to make the rigging process easier. Once the mast has been set into its **"mast step"**, make sure all supporting wires (**shrouds** and **forestay**) are securely fixed into position. Take an extra minute to inspect the fittings, holding the shrouds in place to ensure nothing is loose or in danger of failing. A dismasting, though uncommon, can ruin a good day in a hurry.

Once the mast is up, the sails can be rigged. You may want to fix the boom to the mast (at the gooseneck) now. The **mainsail** is fixed onto the boom with both bottom corners attached securely and tensioned. It's easy to forget to put the **battens** in the mainsail. Without them the sail will stretch and flap constantly, *adding years to the age of a sail in a few hours of sailing*. Make sure they are inserted properly because when the sail flaps, they have a tendency to jump out.

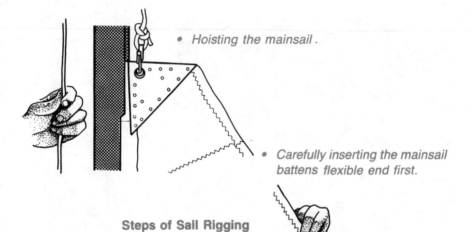

• *Hoisting the mainsail .*

• *Carefully inserting the mainsail battens flexible end first.*

Steps of Sail Rigging

• *Attaching the tack of the mainsail to its fitting near the gooseneck.*

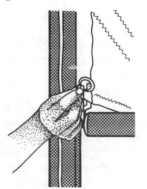

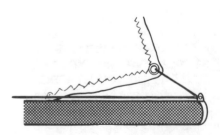

• *Attaching the outhaul to the clew.*

When attaching the main halyard make sure that both ends are untwisted and not wrapped around the mast.

At this point we may want to attach the **main halyard** (rope or wire that hoists the sail) to the top or head of the sail using some variety of **shackle** or rope knot. Check to see that the mainsail is not twisted or wrapped around the boom. Also make sure the **mainsheet** is rigged properly to the boom and boat with no twists, free to run. Proceed to raise the sail. When the sail reaches the top, tension the halyard to eliminate wrinkles in the luff and secure the halyard. Next we can rig the **jib** by attaching the forward corner (tack) to the bow fitting. The **jib sheets** can be tied onto the back corner (clew) and rigged through the proper blocks, fairleads, or cleats on the deck. The **halyard** may now be attached to the head of the sail. Whenever you attach any halyard make sure you look up and follow its path along the mast. *By pulling the halyard taut and away from the mast you can easily see any wraps* or tangles which can and should be unwound before attaching it to the sail.

Make sure the rudder is secure so that it will stay attached even when capsized.

Draining the boat is important before and after sailing.

Finally, *check and drain all watertight compartments* taking special care to secure the plugs, covers or flaps that prevent water from entering the boat or compartments.

You are now almost ready to launch the boat. It's time to make sure that the **centerboard, rudder** and **tiller** are aboard along with extra **life jackets** (PFD's, Personal Flotation Devices), **bailer** or bucket, and any other gear you may want to take with you. Ensure that this extra gear is securely stowed.

If your boat is in a parking lot, take a look around to identify any **power wires** that could touch your mast while moving the boat to the launching site. Also, power lines might go over the water. So keep your eyes open when sailing. If there are any wires nearby take the time when you come ashore to contact the local authorities who should be urged to move them underground or away from the boat launching area.

Your launching situation will dictate your next few minutes of activity. It may be prudent to put on any special clothing, *foulweather gear or wetsuit* now before launching.

We will discuss proper clothing later, but let's talk about life jackets now. I don't care whether you are an Olympic swimmer or not; *it is smart to wear a lifejacket* (PFD) when sailing. It's sort of like wearing seat belts. You may never need them but it is foolish to leave them unworn. Now be wary. There are a lot of different life jackets on the market and you want one that is **COMFORTABLE!** Ask your instructor what life jacket he or she recommends and then shop around. You might as well purchase one now and if you have one that you like you will be more inclined to wear it. Remember, *comfort and mobility* should be the determining factors in its selection.

Smart sailors always wear their life jackets.

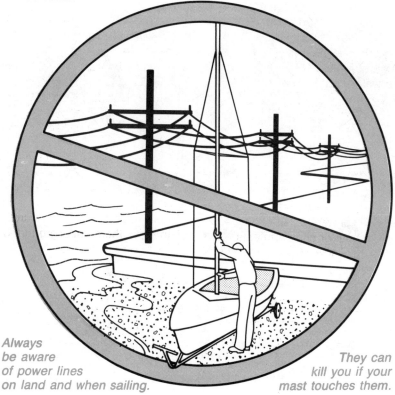

Always be aware of power lines on land and when sailing.

They can kill you if your mast touches them.

Launching

Although boats are well constructed to handle the stresses of sailing they must be *handled carefully* on shore. If you are launching off a ramp or beach you will be using either a trailer or manpower to float the boat. I always try to enlist *more than enough people* if the boat must be carried. It makes it easier for all involved. Once the boat is afloat you must choose the spot where you will hoist sails. Your goal is to find a location where the boat can be held *bow pointing into the wind* while the sails are hoisted, and rudder and centerboard put in place. If you are fortunate, there will be a nearby dock or buoy on which to tie up. If not, you will have to enlist the services of your crew or a helpful onlooker to wade into the water and hold the bow of your boat while sails are hoisted.

If you are launching off the beach never leave the boat half in and half out of the water. Any wave action will hurt the hull by grinding it on the beach or even float the boat away. If there are big waves or surf *avoid standing between the boat and the beach*. Just as a surfer would, keep the boat pointed perpendicular to the waves so they cannot push the hull so hard.

29

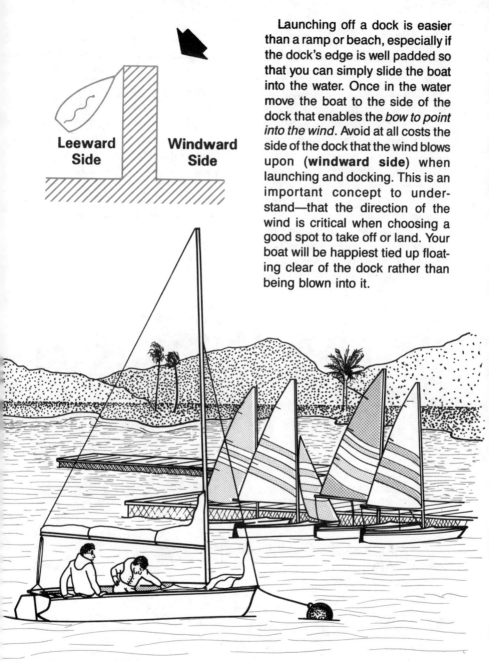

Leeward Side

Windward Side

Launching off a dock is easier than a ramp or beach, especially if the dock's edge is well padded so that you can simply slide the boat into the water. Once in the water move the boat to the side of the dock that enables the *bow to point into the wind*. Avoid at all costs the side of the dock that the wind blows upon (**windward side**) when launching and docking. This is an important concept to understand—that the direction of the wind is critical when choosing a good spot to take off or land. Your boat will be happiest tied up floating clear of the dock rather than being blown into it.

Boats should always be pointed into the wind when launching, sitting at the dock or hoisting sails.

Getting Going:

Now that your boat is in the water it is time to get in the boat and hoist the sails. If your boat is tied to a dock make sure that it is tied securely with a good knot. (See the section on knots for your many choices). A "good knot" is one that is easily untied even after being tensioned hard.

If you have ever stepped into a canoe or rowboat you will know how tippy they can be. A centerboard boat can also be pretty unstable so *step into the boat carefully, trying to keep your weight low and on the centerline*. Once in the boat slide the centerboard or daggerboard down all the way. If you are launching off a beach it may be too shallow to do this, so simply put it down almost until it touches bottom. (Once you sail into deeper water you can slide it down the rest of the way.) This underwater fin will steady the boat and make it easier for you to move around and hoist the sails.

Small boats are tippy, so keep your weight low and on the centerline when boarding the boat.

31

The next step is to put the rudder on and attach the tiller. You are now ready to hoist the sails. It's really your choice as to which sail to hoist first. You may find it easiest to put up the mainsail last so that the swinging boom won't hamper your movement in the boat. Both **main** and **jib** halyards (ropes or wires with which you hoist the sails) should be pulled up *tightly* and cleated securely. Once the sails are up you should get going soon to avoid excessive flapping of the sails. If you do have to stay tied up for a short while make sure the sails' control ropes (**sheets**) are free to run so the sail will not fill and push the boat into the dock.

When leaving a mooring, pull the boat forward using the line attached to the mooring buoy (mooring line) to get the boat moving. Once you have speed enough to steer the boat, release the mooring line.

These are the three common types of PFD's. Make sure to pick one that is comfortable and best suits your sailing needs.

Your First Sail

Once under way you are set free by the wind. It is a great feeling to cast off all ties with the shore. Hopefully, you have a good day and start out with nice medium winds. If the wind is so light that there are barely any ripples on the water don't bother going out. Light air can be very challenging but it is really not much fun since the boat can barely move. If the waves are big and there are mostly white caps out on the open water *you may want to wait for the wind to drop before heading out.* Heavy air sailing is really a challenge that is best approached after you have a few good days of medium (5-12 knots) wind under your belt. Your instructor will know if it is an appropriate day for your first sail.

But assuming the conditions are good, let's go sailing. Since you have been regularly noting the wind direction before casting off you should have a really good *feel* for it. The easiest point of sail to start with is a **reach**—sailing across the wind. Pull the sails in (using the mainsheet and jibsheet) so they are not flapping (**luffing**) and get the feel of steering the boat with a tiller by using a *faraway reference point* to gauge your heading. Once the boat gets moving it will be responsive to tiller movement, so keep a "soft" touch on the helm and keep the tiller close to the centerline to avoid a radical turn that would culminate in a coming about or jibing. Notice how the boat *turns toward the wind* (heads up) *if you*

push the tiller down towards the side of the boat the sails are on. Also note that if you let go of the tiller the boat will not go straight, it will turn toward the wind.

You will find that your position in the boat can have a big effect on its speed and tipping (**heeling**). *The first goal is to be comfortable and still be able to control the boat.* For

the driver (helmsman) the best place to sit is on the windward side (the side the wind blows upon) just even with the end of the tiller. This way you can steer with your back hand and hold the mainsheet with your front hand. *Always sit on the windward side for best visibility.* The sails will be hanging over the leeward side and you will *feel* the wind first on your head before it hits the sails. Get into the habit of using the tiller extension (**hiking stick**) all the time. You will find that using it allows you to sit in the most comfortable position. That's what it's all about, right?

The crew(s) can be placed forward of the driver so that the boat is *sailing with little or no heel.* If it

34

is windy, the crew will sit out on the side with you. If it is light air, they may have to sit on the leeward side to counteract the skipper's weight.

Once you have the feel of how the boat turns it is time to look up at the sails. You will develop a habit of looking up at the sails regularly to see how they are trimmed. In fact the driver's (helmsman) attention should be *constantly rotating between the sails, the water ahead of the boat, and the wind direction.*

If you hold a steady course on a **beam reach** the rudiments of sail trim will come easily. Simply let the sail out until it begins to flap (luff) and then pull it in until it just stops luffing. The sail will appear to be *stable, full of wind.* In fact, if you keep pulling the sail in tighter it will continue to look the same—stable and full of wind. However, for best performance you want the sail to be *trimmed right to the edge so that if you were to let it out any more, it*

Your boat will sail best with crew weight positioned in the middle of the boat, even with the centerboard. Many new sailors sit too far back in the boat. This will slow the boat and looks funny.

35

would begin to luff. Practice this with the mainsail and then the jib until you have gotten a good feel for sail trim. If it is luffing pull it in. If it looks full try easing it out slowly. *Every inch you can ease the sail before luffing will really help*.

Universal Rule: "Let the sails out as far as they can go without luffing".

Congratulations! You have now learned how to sail. Now all you have to do is refine these basic techniques of steering and sail trim. Once you have the beam reach under control try heading up to a **close reach** and then heading down to a **broad reach** and retrimming the sails appropriately. This is when some yarn tied to the shroud can be really helpful in determining wind direction.

There will be times when you want to stop and collect your thoughts before you try again. Try the "safety position". Simply steer the boat so the wind is coming directly over the side and let the sails luff. You will have to gently push the tiller toward the sail to keep the wind coming directly over the side. When you are ready to sail again, pull in the sails.

Now you are ready to learn the *art of close hauled sailing*.

If you need a break, point the boat on a beam reach and ease out the sails. With the tiller pushed to leeward, the boat will sit happily for hours! This is called the safety position.

"SAFETY POSITION"

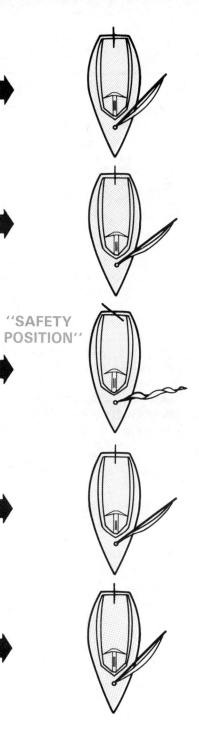

Close Hauled Sailing:

It's really quite easy. You simply sail the boat as close to the wind as possible without luffing. As we learned earlier, this is about 45 degrees to the wind direction. Close-hauled sailing requires *very smooth and accurate steering*. Remember, just keep a nice, easy, light touch on the tiller and try to avoid over steering.

On reaches we adjusted our sail trim to the course of the boat. But sailing close hauled we will trim the sails in tightly (the reason we call it "close hauled") and delicately alter our course to keep the sails just "full". Once you find that **magic groove** where the tightly trimmed sails just begin to luff, you can keep the boat steering very straight with occasional checks to

see that you are still near the "groove".

It's easy to drift off a close hauled course and out of the "groove" if you are not careful. The problem is that the sails will continue to appear "full" and the boat will move (albeit slowly) even if you turn down to a beam reaching course. The solution is to keep the wind direction in your mind's eye and keep checking that you are sailing as close to the wind as possible without luffing the sails.

When you drift off a close hauled course by turning towards the wind you will know in a hurry. The sails will luff and the boat will quickly slow down. Before the boat comes to a stop (remember, without forward motion the boat cannot

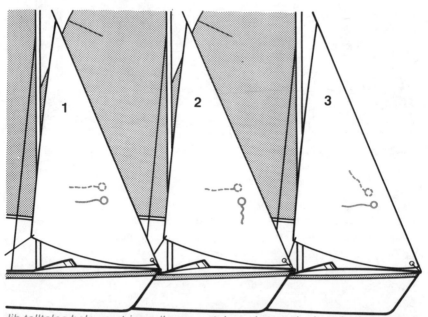

Jib telltales help you trim sails accurately and steer the boat in the upwind groove. Boat 1 has perfect trim with both telltales streaming back. Boat 2 is stalled and must either head up or ease the sail to get the yarns flowing. Boat 3 is "pinching" and must either head down or trim the sail.

be turned), pull the tiller gently toward you (the windward side of the boat) to head down. It shouldn't take much of a turn to get back on course and up to speed.

Another common mistake to avoid is letting the sails out. Since your sail trim constrains how close to the wind your boat can sail, you must *avoid easing them out at all*. The exception to this rule is in windy conditions when you may have to ease and luff the mainsail to avoid excessive tipping (heeling). Even then you should keep the jib in tight and key on it when sailing

in the *close hauled groove*.

Telltales (6 inch pieces of dark yarn) taped to the lower front edge of the sail can help you find and stay in that upwind groove. They work best on a jib when positioned about 30 inches up from the bottom corner (tack) and 6 inches in from the front edge (luff), with one on each side. Essentially, they are more accurate indicators of the wind flow over the sail than waiting for it to actually luff. To tell you the truth, I find it very difficult to sail a good close hauled course without telltales.

Coming About/Tacking

Sight across the boat at 90 degrees to your heading before you tack to see where you will be headed and see that the course is clear.

Move tiller to leeward. The bow will turn through the wind and the sails will fill on the other side. Release the jibsheet and trim in the other side.

You must work out a method of changing hands between mainsheet and tiller depending on the sheeting arrangements.

Close hauled sailing is especially exciting because you can now go anywhere on the water. By changing tacks (**coming about or tacking**) once or twice *you can sail your boat to a destination that is directly upwind*. Christopher Columbus would have been envious. Coming about is an easy maneuver. It will require a fairly big turn (about 90 degrees) from one close hauled course to the other. The driver must also change sides of the boat during the "tack" so as to steer from the new windward side. In a boat with a jib the crew will work together with the skipper by also changing sides of the boat while shifting the jib from one side to the other.

It will help to pick a point on the windward (toward the wind) horizon that you guess is about 90 degrees from the close hauled course you are presently steering. Keep your eyes on this point to avoid over or understeering during the turn. Prior to coming about you should prepare your crew by saying something like the traditional *"ready about"*. At that point, they may want to uncleat the jib, hold it tight with their hands and respond "ready". As you begin your turn you could announce by saying, *"tacking"* or the traditional *"hard a lee"* (referring to the motion of pushing the tiller to leeward). When the boat is pointed directly toward the wind you can begin to cross the boat. It's sort of like learning a dance step because you must keep one hand on the tiller passing it behind you and one on the mainsheet

As the sails come across on the new tack they should be trimmed in almost as far as before and brought into the ideal position as soon as the boat is up to full speed.

Tacking is a matter of timing, teamwork and practice. Since the boat is slowing as you turn into the wind , you must learn to quickly come about from one tack to the other with a minimum loss of speed.

as you cross sides. With some practice you will be doing it smoothly every time. The crew must watch and tend to the jib. When it begins to luff the *"old"* jib sheet should be released and the *"new"* one trimmed in and cleated an instant later.

It takes some practice to make a smooth tack every time, but I can think of no better place to be working on it than out on the water.

You may want to exercise your or your crew's brains a little by considering on what tack the boat is sailing (port or starboard). It's good practice. The only thing left to cover during your first or second sail is the point of sail called **"running"** and changing tacks by **jibing**.

Here are several commonly made mistakes you should avoid when coming about:

- Not turning the boat far enough and getting stuck **"in irons"**.

- Turning the boat **too far** so it ends up on a reach instead of close hauled on the new tack.

- The crew **forgetting to change jib sheets** and ending up with the jib being trimmed tightly by the windward jib sheet.

- Not changing sides or ending up in some contorted, ridiculous looking position.

Running—Sailing Downwind

Running **downwind** or **broad reaching** is a great point of sail. It's probably my favorite, especially when it is windy. The phrase: *"Broad Reaching Through Life"* says it all. The boat really surfs along on the waves and because the wind is from behind, you rarely get wet. The only problem is that for every foot you sail downwind you end up having to sail upwind 1.4 feet to get back to where you started. (Just picture an isoceles right triangle to see what I mean.) I must admit that it is really difficult to distinguish between a broad reach and a running course. In both cases, *the wind is more or less straight behind the boat* and I find that I often merge the two in my mind. Sail trim is pretty simple on a run. Just let the mainsail out all the way until it hits the shroud or when the boom is perpendicular to the course, if the boat has no shrouds. The jib will not be very effective on a run since the mainsail blocks most of its wind. For fun you may want to try to *"wing it"* by holding it out on the opposite side from the main. However, without some sort of pole to keep it out there you may find that it is more trouble than it is worth.

You will find that on a run you can sit more inside the boat to keep it upright. There are a couple of fine points to go over. First, your centerboard or daggerboard, which was doing a lot of work preventing side-slip when sailing close hauled, is not so necessary sailing downwind. You can raise it *a little more than halfway* to get some extra speed; just don't forget to lower it when going back upwind.

Practice triangle course.

In fact, if you want to see something humorous pull your centerboard up *all the way* when you are sailing along *close hauled*. The boat will keep pointing in the same direction, but it will be slipping sideways so fast you will never get anywhere upwind.

Another fine point is the use of a rigging device known as the **boom vang**. When sailing downwind in medium or strong breeze the boom vang rope should be tensioned to *keep the boom from soaring way up in the air*. By keeping the boom down the back edge (leech) of the mainsail can stay straight just like a wing. You can even use the boom vang on reaches.

"Winging" the jib on a run.

Steering

Finally, let's discuss steering. As noted earlier, you have a bit more flexibility when steering downwind compared with the accuracy needed for keeping it in the groove sailing close hauled. However, there is one exception—**avoid sailing by the lee**. By using your face or a piece of yarn on the shrouds you can track the wind direction and avoid the potential danger of an accidental jibe when sailing by the lee. No matter which direction you are sailing, *watching the horizon* will help you to stay *oriented* and *avoid oversteering*.

Choose a course that will take you most directly to your destination, keeping in mind the wind direction and points of sail. You will find that when the boat heels too much it will become difficult to hold the boat on a straight course. So avoid excess heeling when it's important to sail a steady course.

Jibing

Jibing is the alternative method to coming about for changing tacks. Your choice of whether to come about or jibe will most likely be dictated by your heading. If you are sailing along on a broad reach or run then it's probably easiest to jibe. The steering part of a jibe is simple because you don't have to go through a "no sail zone". Remember to check your new heading to be sure the course is clear. If your boat is going directly downwind you could, in fact, *jibe without turning at all* by simply throwing the boom over to the other side. The key is getting the boom across smoothly from one side to the other.

It can be a simple matter of pulling the mainsheet in all of the way and then letting it out again on the other side. This is a *controlled jibe* since the boom does not come crashing across. I like pulling in the mainsail about halfway and letting the wind do the rest by steering so far by the lee that the wind pushes the sail across. No matter how you

A jibe is a turn downwind that brings the stern through the wind. During a jibe the boom swings rapidly from one side of the boat to the other.

In this sequence the sailor jibes the boat from starboard tack (stages 1, 2, & 3) to port tack (stage 4). The sailor changes sides and steering hands as the boom comes swinging across blown by the full force of the wind (stages 3 & 4).

do it remember to **keep your head low!**

Prepare your crew by saying something like *"ready to jibe"* and at the moment the boom starts across say *"jibing"* or the more traditional *"jibe-ho"*. The crew's responsibility is to keep the boat upright and stay low. The crew can also switch tension to the new jib sheet. Remember, *the jibsheet in use should always be on the same side as the mainsail and boom.*

A word of warning. In stronger winds the jibe is a tricky maneuver. What was in light air a mellow matter of throwing the boom across can become a real bear in strong winds. The possibility of a capsize, although always present in a centerboard boat, is at its highest during a heavy air jibe. So there is no one who will fault you if you decide to come about in lieu of jibing. Remember, *you never have to jibe.* But you can always come about instead. As you gain more experience and confidence you will be able to jibe in stronger and stronger winds.

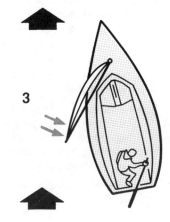

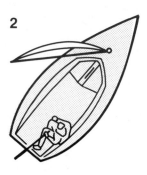

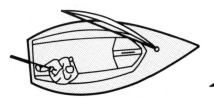

A Smart Sailor's Safety Considerations

- **Always wear a lifejacket** (PFD). Buy your own which fits and is really comfortable.

- Always consider the **weather forecast** before sailing.

- Set an **upper limit for wind velocity** for your sailing. You have plenty of time to slowly raise that limit as you gain more experience.

- **Dress appropriately**. Remember that it can be a lot colder on the water no matter how warm it is on shore.

- Be sure of your **ability to right the boat** in case of a capsize. Make sure your buckets or bailers are tied into the boat so they will not float away.

- Always make sure your **rudder will not fall out** if the boat turns upside down. There are many fancy systems such as spring clips to keep the rudder attached but a simple rope tied on works well, too.

- The above rule also applies to daggerboards.

- Always check and **drain the tanks** and hull before sailing. Make sure all appropriate drain holes are tightly sealed.

- Always **keep a good lookout** especially in the "blind" spot to leeward underneath the boom.

- The Navy recommends: Whenever the combination of air and water temperatures is less than 120 degrees a wetsuit or other protection is required.

- Never stand between a floating boat and the shore if there are any waves.

- Make sure you have some way to get the boat ashore if the wind dies. Paddles work well on larger boats. You may be able to paddle with your hands on a smaller boat. A good trick is aggressively rocking the boat back and forth with the sails trimmed in tightly, "creating" your own wind.

- Never go sailing when there are no other boats out.

- If the water temperature is below 60 degrees you should seriously consider wearing a **drysuit** or **wetsuit**. They could save your life and they are very comfortable.

- Don't forget to **duck** when you **jibe!**

- Keep your **hands** and **fingers in the boat** when coming alongside a dock or another boat.

- Head to shore immediately if you hear **thunder** or see **lightning**.

- If you capsize and cannot right the boat, **stay with the boat**. Try to get out of the water by sitting on the overturned hull and wait for help.

Review Questions

1. Of all the following, what does not need to be done prior to sailing? (Choose one)

   a) Make sure you have your PFD and other sailing gear
   b) Keep your eye out for power lines when rigging and moving your boat
   c) Inspect the fittings holding the mast and shrouds in place
   d) Make sure sails are completely dry
   e) Make sure hull and buoyancy tanks are drained and plugged tightly

2. Why do you want to tie up the boat at a dock so that it points directly towards the wind? (Note: Choose all correct answers)

   a) So that no one can hit your boat
   b) To make it easy to hoist your sails
   c) So that the boat does not hit the dock while you are rigging the sails
   d) It is the best spot from which to start sailing
   e) It is easiest to start sailing on a run

3. Answer the following True or False

   a) Jib and Main halyards should never be pulled tight.   T   F
   b) Main and Jib sheets should never be cleated when the boat is sitting at the dock   T   F
   c) Winds over 15 knots are recommended for your first sail   T   F
   d) The driver should always sit on the windward side   T   F
   e) As long as a sail is not luffing, then it is properly trimmed   T   F
   f) Once you select a sail trim you never change it   T   F

4. The difference in sail trim between close hauled sailing and all other points of sail is: (choose the one BEST answer)

   a) When sailing close hauled you keep the sails trimmed tightly (except in strong breezes) and steer carefully to keep them from luffing
   b) The sail does not luff when sailing close hauled
   c) The sail generates more power when sailing close hauled
   d) You do not have to look up at the luff of the sail when sailing close hauled
   e) It is easier to do

Safe Sailing

Capsizes:

Capsizing is a part of sailing centerboard boats. It can be a nuisance, but it should never be feared. Given proper preparation and practice it can be handled easily. Although a capsize can be frustrating, it can also be fun. If the water is warm you may appreciate the welcome chance to cool off.

Sooner or later you are going to "flip", so why not now? A *capsize drill* should be part of your first course in sailing unless the conditions or boat make it impractical.

With the boat flipped upside down all of the loose gear in the boat will float away, so plan ahead and make sure everything is well

Capsizing is safe and can be fun.

ONE IMPORTANT RULE: Always stay with the boat if you capsize even if you have problems righting it. Don't try to swim to shore. By staying with the boat you can be seen better, float longer and will be rescued sooner.

stowed or tied into the boat just in case. There are basically two types of centerboard boats with respect to capsizing: those that can be righted and sailed dry (*self-righting* and *self-bailing*) and those that *"swamp"* or fill up with water and require outside assistance to bail out. The difference is in the design of the boat and whether it sports sealed flotation tanks. As a rule, you should *avoid sailing in a "swamper" if there is no rescue boat available*.

The Anatomy of a Capsize.

There are two ways a boat can capsize while sailing: by tipping over to *leeward* or to *windward*. A leeward capsize is common in strong or puffy winds when the boat simply "blows over" because the crew did not sit out on the side (**hike**) and/or **ease the mainsheet enough**. (See the section on heavy air sailing for more detail on keeping the boat upright.)

Capsizing to leeward. The sailor should have eased the mainsheet in the puff to reduce heel.

"The Death Roll"
Capsizing to windward.

To prevent rolling over the
sailor should have headed up
slightly and trimmed in the mainsheet.

When the boat flips to leeward the crew's first reaction is to stay dry and climb over the high side and onto the centerboard. This is called the **walkover method**. This is the proper reaction but it must be done quickly. *Most boats do not like to float on their sides*; they prefer to roll belly up with the mast pointing towards China. This ignoble position is known as **"turning turtle"**. If you can get onto the centerboard quickly when the boat is still lying on its side you will be able to prevent the turtle. But if you spend too much time climbing over the side you will accelerate the turtling process. The other choice, and sometimes it's not a choice, is to jump into the water and swim around to the exposed center-board. This is when you will be happy that you are wearing a life jacket because it is difficult to swim with your clothes on.

The other common capsize scenario is going over the other way—to windward. This will occur in strong winds when sailing down-wind, especially during a jibe. The boat just starts rolling back and forth and finally, crash...the **"death roll"**. A death roll can be avoided by *heading up to a reach*, turning the boat toward the wind and *trimming in the mainsheet*. But once the boat rolls over it is really tough to stay dry and your only choice is to swim around and climb on the centerboard.

Righting the Boat

Now you are faced with the task of righting the boat. Make certain that *the sheets are free to run and your crew is safe and happy.* Simply climb on the centerboard and use your weight on the lever arm provided by the centerboard to bring the boat upright. If the mainsheet and jibsheet are uncleated, then the boat should stay upright while you pull yourself in. This is the case if you lever the boat upright with the mast downwind (to leeward).

If you try to pull the boat up with the mast to windward (often the case after a death roll) the wind will lift the sail and *flip the boat over on top of you.* If you have a free crew member he can keep the boat from blowing over by positioning himself on the opposite side of the boat to you and holding it upright. But if you are singlehanded you may have to pull the old underwater move. As the mast blows up and over, hold onto your breath and the centerboard. You will end up with the boat on its side and the mast pointed downwind where you want it. Now you can bring it upright and climb in.

Righting the boat. Be patient and let your body weight slowly lever the sail out of the water. Make sure the sheets are released and free to run so the boat doesn't sail away from you.

During this process the crew can help out by keeping an eye on the righting process. One very effective technique is to *hold onto the bow*. The boat will naturally drift with the wind until the bow is pointed directly upwind. Another effective method is to have a crew member go to the mast tip and help the boat around. This makes it easy for the other crew member to bring the boat upright and climb in. Some-times if the boat turns turtle it is difficult to get it back on its side with only one person pulling on the board. The other crew can provide more righting force by climbing up and leaning out while holding onto the waist of their friend.

NOTE: Sudden gusts cause a capsize. To avoid a capsize, sail with the mainsheet uncleated, ready to release it to spill a sudden gust.

Scoop Recovery Method

One very effective way to right a two person, self-rescuing dinghy has been developed in San Francisco Bay by two 100 lb. sailors who blast around in strong 20 knot summer-time breezes. When the boat capsizes first make sure it is not going to turn turtle by climbing onto the centerboard and leveraging the mast until it is nearly out of the water. Then the crew swims around to the cockpit and releases all cleats holding the jib or mainsail. The crew gets between the boom and the hull and throws the high jib sheet to the skipper. The skipper is up on the centerboard watching the crew so that they always talk to and see one another. After the crew has freed the sheets he grabs onto the hiking straps in the cockpit and says "Go for it". The skipper, using the high jib sheet thrown up to him for leverage, leans back and raises the mast out of the water. The crew, lying in the bottom of the boat holding onto the hiking strap, gets "scooped" into the boat. Once the boat is upright the crew helps the skipper in over the transom while all the sails are luffing.

1. *Quickly swim around to centerboard and make sure boat does not "turtle".*

2. Crew throws high jibsheet to skipper.

3. Skipper uses jibsheet to right boat.

4. Crew is "SCOOPED" into the boat.

Rescuing the "Swamper"

Boats that are not self-rescuing are much more time consuming to get sailing again. First you must lower the sails and then bring the boat upright by pulling on the centerboard. Now you are faced with a big job of bailing. One way to do it is with a big bucket. The idea is to climb into the boat over the transom so it doesn't flip again and start bailing like crazy. If you are fast and keep the boat upright, you can slowly gain on the flood waters and get it dry. If there is an opening on top of the centerboard trunk, consider stuffing a towel into the opening to stop the upward flow of water. But be forewarned, *a boat half filled with water is very unstable* and will flip again rather easily.

A much easier way is the **"quick tow"** with the aid of a motor boat. A motor boat with a well-secured tow rope can slowly pull the boat so that the water flows out over the back end (transom). You must stay in the water holding on to the back end to keep the boat steady while the tow is effected. Soon the water level will be down to a level that can be bailed out with your bucket.

One thing is for certain. *Never sail a non-self-rescuing sailboat alone with no other boats around.* And always make sure there is a good bucket or two aboard in case you do flip.

Heavy Air Sailing

Sailing in strong breezes (15-25 knots) can be an exhilarating experience in a small boat. There is nothing quite like the feeling of **planing** (surfing) along, inches above the water, with spray blasting all around the hull. *Heavy air sailing requires practice.* If you are a beginner avoid these stronger breezes until you have built some experience in the light and moderate breezes under 15 knots. It won't take long to feel confident in stronger breezes. Then you will relish windy days rather than feel uncomfortable whenever white caps blow up. *Never sail a boat in heavy air unless you are sure that you and your crew can right it from a capsize.*

Upwind and Close Reaching

On these "tighter" points of sail the real challenge is to try to minimize the heeling forces of the wind on the sails. You have *three weapons* in your "anti-heel" arsenal. First there is your own body weight. Leaning out with your butt hanging over the windward side of the boat is a very effective way to reduce heel. The hiking stick and mainsheet can help provide support. Some boats have straps under which you can hook your toes to help you **"hike out"** farther. Many catamarans and some high performance single hull boats have a **trapeze system**. This is a very efficient method of countering the forces of

the wind on the sails. Trapeze boats are usually very fast in strong breezes because they make the best use of the crew's weight. However, no matter what kind of boat you are on, you and your crew must sit on the windward side when sailing close hauled in heavy air. It is the single most effective tool you have to keep the boat sailing along in strong winds.

Another anti-heel device is **steering**. By turning the boat slightly closer to the wind you can reduce the pressure on the sails, thereby reducing heel. This technique is called **"pinching"** or **"feathering"**.

The key is to accurately control the heading of the boat with your rudder. You will find that through *very small course adjustments* (under 3 degrees) you will be able to accurately control heel.

When using this technique you will find that the sails may just begin to flap (luff) along their leading edges but the back half of the sails should remain "full". Pinching can be taken too far, to the extreme where the sails are fully luffing. This must be avoided since without any sail power the boat will stop.

Another similar way to "bleed off" or reduce some pressure when sailing upwind or close reaching is by holding a constant course while **easing the mainsheet**. This must be done controllably until the heel is reduced to an acceptable amount (under 10 degrees for a centerboard boat). The beauty of this system is that it is very quick. If your boat has

a jib, it can be left full and driving while the constantly adjusted mainsail balances the boat. When sailing upwind it is best to *keep the mainsheet in your hand* for fast reaction.

By using a combination of these techniques you will be able to sail close-hauled very efficiently even in strong winds. The goal is to settle on *an acceptable amount of heel angle* (around 10 degrees) and then keep the boat sailing along with good speed at that angle. Your own internal sense of balance can easily sense minute changes in the boat's heel angle which you can counter by steering, mainsail trim or hiking out farther.

It is important to control the angle of heel of your boat. This boat is heeling too much, 10 degrees is a good maximum for speed and safety. The mainsheet should be eased to "spill" some power out of the sail.

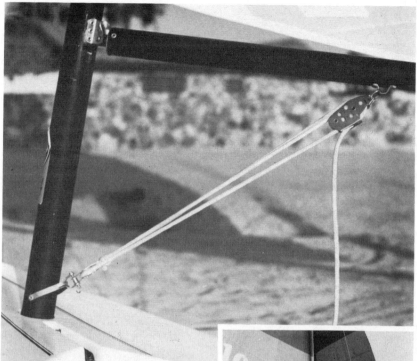

Proper tensioning of the boom vang will lower the boom, increase efficiency and help control the boat.

Downwind

Downwind sailing in strong breezes is a real joy. Beam reaching and broad reaching are fast and exhilarating. You may want to avoid sailing straight with the wind on a run since the boat is most prone to a "death roll" on this course. The boom vang, mentioned earlier as a mainsail adjustment, is especially important when sailing downwind in strong breezes since it keeps the boom from rising, thereby keeping the mainsail in a nice wing shape which inhibits rolling.

Notice: running without a boom vang makes the boom rise and is inefficient.

Man Overboard

It does happen. For one reason or a combination of reasons, someone who didn't want to "goes swimming". On a small boat getting the swimmer aboard can be done quickly. You've learned how to bring a person back aboard during your capsize recovery, that is, over the tramsom or possibly the weather side where the wind can help balance the boat.

When practicing the overboard recovery techniques using a cushion, first keep in mind it is important to get the boat under control, then yell "man overboard", keep the "swimmer" in sight, and safely and quickly approach the swimmer from leeward. Quickly getting back to your swimmer is important and possible methods are diagramed here.

The Figure-eight method stresses the importance of keeping the boat under control and gives the novice time to approach the swimmer safely. The Quick Stop method stresses the importance of staying in the immediate area of the swimmer. In this method the boat is immediately tacked, leaving the jib cleated. You should experiment with this last method on your boat. In heavy winds this method can lead to a capsize.

Also shown is an optional light air method involving a jibe to get downwind of the swimmer. Which method you choose will depend on conditions and your own boat handling skill. "Man Overboard" practice is very important and can be fun.

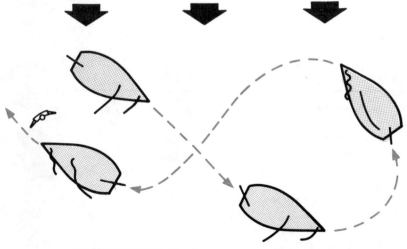

"FIGURE 8" Method

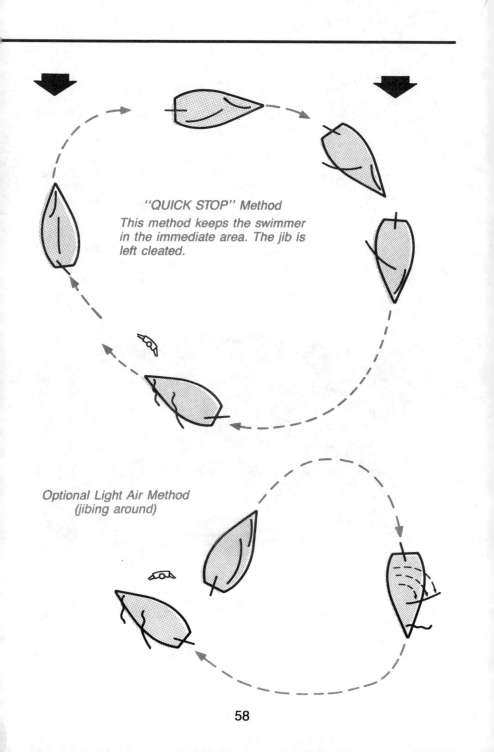

"QUICK STOP" Method

This method keeps the swimmer in the immediate area. The jib is left cleated.

Optional Light Air Method (jibing around)

What to Wear

Small boat sailing can be really wet. As sailors we should be more concerned with the **"wind chill"** factor than air temperature. Shorts and a T-shirt may be the most comfortable shoreside attire on many summer days but out on the water the effect of the wind and the water on your body can cool you off in a hurry. Fortunately, there are a lot of good articles of clothing designed specifically for the sailor and outdoor enthusiast that can keep you comfortable in just about any condition. Color of your clothing and foul weather gear is important.

Reds and oranges are very visible at sea, whereas blues and whites are not and tend to make a person overboard very difficult to sight.

Let's start with your feet. Even on the warmest of days it is best to wear a pair of shoes to facilitate movement in the boat and protect yourself against injury from objects on the deck, aboard the boat and in the water. There are a zillion "boat shoes" with non-skid rubber soles on the market. But I have found that any old pair of sneakers or running shoes work just as well.

Rubber boots or neoprene windsurfing shoes keep your feet warm in colder conditions. Your socks should be made of wool, polypropolene or thermax (two popular names for a family of synthetic fibers with incredible insulation power even when wet).

On many summer days you can wear the same clothes you would on shore. However, it's a good idea to bring along a *windbreaker* or *nylon shell* just in case things get cool. I always pack a lightweight jacket like this in my duffel bag since it can be somewhat water resistant on days when you only occasionally get a little spray.

Dry suits are very popular in colder weather. They are worn over your regular clothing and will keep you dry even in the event of a capsize.

Dealing with the Cold

Other than your personal life jacket (PFD) which is selected for its comfort, the first piece of sail clothing you will need is some "foul weather gear". This is very important when sailing in cold weather or on cold water.

This gear comes in a variety of weights, sizes and shapes, but its one purpose is to keep you dry, and therefore, warm. Ask your instructor what he/she recommends if you are unsure what to buy. I really like "one-piece" foul weather gear jump-suits because they provide good mobility and are simple to bring along. They can get too warm, so a lighter weight two-piece suit might be better for you and your local area.

For boardsailing and real wet-weather sailing a more appropriate item may be a **wet-suit** or **dry-suit**. Again, ask your instructor for advice on these specialty items.

In cold weather you will want to have good insulation underneath your foul weather gear. Sailors are constantly faced with the dilemma of how to stay warm yet still mobile. Like socks, the layers under the foul weather gear should provide good insulation even when wet. This rules out cotton clothing and makes the new, man-made fibers like poly-propolene and thermax or the old standby, wool, very attractive.

Hypothermia

Hypothermia is a condition that you unfortunately may experience on the water. It is when your internal body temperature drops below 95 degrees F. Symptoms of mild hypothermia include feeling cold, violent shivering and slurred speech. Treatment includes wrapping the person in warm blankets and giving him/her warm fluids (no alcohol). Symptoms of medium hypothermia include pale appearance, blue lips, severe shivering, headache, loss of muscular control, drowsiness, and incoherence. This is very serious. A person with medium hypothermia needs to be immediately taken out of the cold and reheated. The best thing one can do to prevent hypothermia is to dress warmly. It may be warm on the dock or beach, but it's another situation out on the water in the spray and wind. Be prepared.

SYMPTOMS OF HYPOTHERMIA

1. Pale appearance

2. Blue lips

3. Listlessness

4. Severe shivering

Dealing with the Sun

Most sailing is done in the warmer climes where we can leave our foulweather gear ashore or rolled up in a plastic garbage bag to stay dry in the cockpit. However, *the harmful effects of the sun's ultraviolet rays are increased by the reflection off the sails and the water*. Don't take any chances with your skin—a sunburn can ruin a nice day on the water. I always wear a visor and sunglasses with lenses that provide ultraviolet protection. I always apply **maximum protection, water resistant sunblock** cream (sun protection factor, SPF, of 15 or greater) on my face and often wear light-colored, cotton longsleeve shirts and pants to give my skin a break from the sun. Cotton clothing allows you to perspire, thus helping to avoid heat exhaustion. Heat exhaustion occurs when your body can't control its own temperature. Bright sunshine and high

humidity cause heat exhaustion. If you feel sick, dizzy, tired or develop a headache, find help and a place to cool off. Your body cools itself through perspiration, therefore, drink plenty of water to replace the fluids lost by sweating. Just remember that the sun can do more than give you a St. Tropez tan.

The only other specialty sailing item you may want to consider is a pair of **sailing gloves**. They will protect your hands from chafing on the lines. However, these gloves are easily misplaced and once you develop toughness on your hands a little chafe from ropes is not too bad. I recommend keeping a pair of gloves around for the first few sails of the season and then filing them away for next year.

Five Rules of Good Sailing

These five rules were developed by Sailing Instructors of the Northwestern University Shields Sailing Club in Chicago. It was found that whenever a sailing student was having difficulty, one of these five rules was not being followed.

1. **PREPARE:** Prepare yourself, your boat and your crew.
2. **CONTROL:** Control yourself, your boat and your crew.
3. **INSPECT:** Inspect, inspect, and reinspect.
4. & 5. A **NEAT** and **CLEAN** ship is a safe and happy ship.

You will find it valuable to review any difficulties or problem areas with your sailing instructor in the format of these five rules. They will help you better organize your thoughts and attitudes.

Review Questions

1. Answer the following statements True or False

a) You should never practice capsizing in your boat because you know how to avoid capsizing   T   F

b) Never sail a Swamper without rescue boats around   T   F

c) Always cleat the mainsheet before righting your boat   T   F

d) You should cleat the mainsheet when sailing in heavy air because that's when it pulls the hardest   T   F

e) It is good to sail with a lot of heel in strong winds   T   F

f) Always bring an extra layer of clothing along in case it gets cooler on the water   T   F

g) You always stay dry on a sailboat if you keep it heeled enough   T   F

2. Which of the following are effective methods of reducing heel when sailing upwind in strong breezes (choose all correct answers)

a) Using a steering technique known as "pinching"

b) Hiking out over the rail

c) Sailing only on the tack that takes you towards land

d) Easing the jib sheet and keeping the main in tight

e) Easing the mainsheet and keeping the jib in tight

Advanced Topics

Crewing

Many centerboard boats are designed to handle the extra weight and help of additional crew. Even a boat designed to be sailed by one person can be fun for two people. Just be careful not to excessively overload any boat no matter what its size.

Crewing on two-man and three-man boats requires active participation in handling the boat. The crew will be responsible for watching out for other boats and the *jib sail* if there is one, and may have other duties such as *hiking out, adjusting the centerboard, helping to launch and dock the boat, and having fun!*.

Once sailing it is especially important to be conscious of your position in the boat. You must be seated in front of the driver but *your side to side (athwartships) position is especially critical.* In our section on sailing in strong winds we discuss the importance of sitting out on the windward side to counteract the tipping (heeling) forces of the wind on the sails. Because the crew does not have to steer, they are in a better position to really sit out far over the side using the jib sheet and hiking straps for additional support. This is a good position to watch the jib telltales and be alert to other boats and objects ahead. Remember to keep your body well positioned. Keep your hands and feet together. This makes your movements more effective. In less wind the crew's side to side position is just as important. They should be able to cleat and uncleat the sheets from their position. In general, a *centerboard boat sails best with somewhere between flat (mast straight upward, no heel) and 10 degrees of leeward heel.* Let the driver choose a comfortable position that allows good visibility and then situate your body so that the boat's heeling angle is within the proper bounds.

Jib trim is easy if you follow the rules introduced earlier. Simply stated, the sail must be trimmed (by the jibsheet) so that it looks "full" but is really on the verge of flapping (luffing). The only way to check this out is by *slowly easing the jibsheet until it begins to show a small luff and then pulling it in slightly.* However, when *sailing close hauled,* the

skipper will "test" the trim by turning toward the wind. Simply keep the *jibsheet trimmed in tightly* and cleated for this point of sail.

Changing tacks is an especially active time for the crew. Not only do you have to move to the opposite side of the boat to stay at the proper heel when the wind comes from the opposite side, but you also must shift the tension from one jibsheet to the other. A common mistake for newcomers is to have the jib trimmed with the windward (wrong side) jibsheet. If you get confused with which side is windward and leeward (the jib should always be tensioned with the leeward jibsheet) simply let both jibsheets loose so the sail flaps like a flag. *Pull in the jibsheet on whichever side the jib is flapping.* It will be the proper, leeward sheet. Another way to remember is that the jib is always trimmed on the same side as the mainsail.

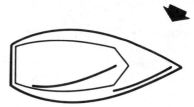

Proper jib trim with jib and mainsail on the same side.

Jib trimmed on wrong side, opposite the mainsail.

Centerboards

Since this book is about small boat sailing we should consider the use of the centerboard or daggerboard. Keel boats with their heavy unadjustable keels are simple since you have no choice; their keels are down all of the time. But centerboard boats are much more fun since they do not have to drag that heavy lead-filled keel around with them and they use movable crew weight to keep the boat upright.

Size, weight, stability and maneuverability are the major differences between the centerboard boat and its larger keel boat brother.

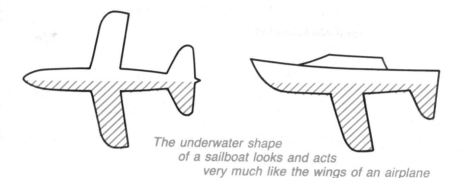

The underwater shape of a sailboat looks and acts very much like the wings of an airplane

When sailing on a close hauled course *the centerboard should be all the way down*, perpendicular to the bottom of the hull. This provides the optimum wing shaped area under the boat to counteract the strong sideways force of the wind and reduce sideslip.

The centerboard counteracts the sideways force created by the sails and allows the boat to move nearly straight forward instead of sliding sideways.

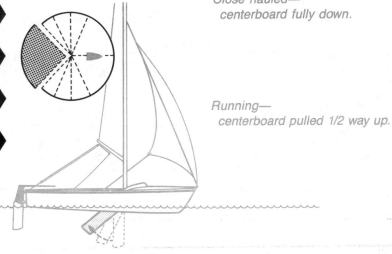

Close hauled—
centerboard fully down.

Running—
centerboard pulled 1/2 way up.

When sailing on a run the board can be raised a little more than half-way because there is little or no sideways force from the sails to worry about. By raising it we are also reducing drag and increasing speed. As you turn closer to the wind from a run you can slowly lower the board until it is all of the way down when you are close hauled. There is really no magic about the board position; and if you forget to pull it up on a reach or a run you probably will not notice the lack of speed.

Planning Your Sail

Once you have learned enough to solo, you will be faced with the decision of where to go on your daysail. There are several factors that you may want to consider when planning your sail. Although some of the best days are when you just "sail around" with no set plan, still you want to keep these points in the back of your mind..

Wind and Weather

It is always best to *check the weather report* before sailing so that you are not caught out in a sudden squall or winds above your skill level. As a sailor, your interest in weather and the marine forecast goes beyond the scope of most TV and newspaper reports. I recommend getting one of those inexpensive *VHF weatherband radios* for your home so that you can plan your sailing days better. Special broadcasts specifically for boaters are updated regularly with useful information on winds and tides, etc.

Plan your day to maximize your chances of a nice sailing breeze and to avoid sailing in stronger winds than you are capable of handling. Many areas of the country experience a *sea breeze* on warm, sunny summer days. This onshore breeze picks up throughout the daylight hours. You may want to plan your sail for the best breeze of the day.

Another consideration is wind direction. If the weather report predicts a strong, southerly sea-breeze in the late afternoon you may want to start your sail earlier in the day and head towards the south. When the strong breeze fills in you will enjoy a comfortable broad reach home rather than slug it out sailing close hauled into the eye of the wind.

Keep your eyes open on the water for threatening weather approaching, such as large thunder head clouds, squall lines, and small white fluffy clouds in front of a dark gray sky, or just a sudden blowing of sand on the beach. Different areas of the country can have different warning signs, so ask your instructor for common signs of bad weather and in what direction to look for them.

Tides and Currents

In certain areas of the planet the tidal range (the rise and fall of the water level) between high and low tides can be as much as 40 feet. This movement of the water is caused by the gravitational force of the moon pulling on the large bodies of water in the ocean. Sailors should be aware if they are sailing in an area with large tidal ranges since it will affect the depth of the water and where they can sail.

Current

Current is the movement of water caused by any number of forces including tides, wind or river flow. Sailing on a current is like walking on a moving sidewalk. It can make you go faster or slower depending on whether you are sailing with or against the current. Use visual signs like the wake around buoys, anchored boats, or floating objects

Boat A: Sailing **with** the current: (Speed over the bottom) = Speed through the water **plus** speed of current

Boat B: Sailing **against** the current: (Speed over the bottom) = Speed through the water **minus** speed of current

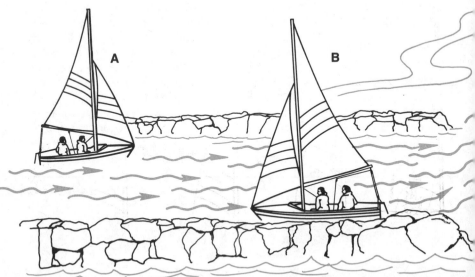

Both boats C & D are trying to make the mouth of the river but a strong tidal current is running from left to right. Boat D is "crabbing up current" to approach the river mouth on a straight line. Boat C, not allowing for the strong cross current, will find itself directly "down stream" of the current with a much longer course to sail.

to determine the direction and speed of the current. If you sail in an area with a strong current, have your instructor point out where and when the current is the strongest. New sailors should never sail in areas with strong currents.

In areas that are affected by **tidal conditions** you will want to be wary of the *direction of the current* and how it may change during your sail. One of the more frustrating ex-periences for a sailor is to be caught "downcurrent" in light air, fighting against the current to get home through a channel.

Another factor to consider in tidal waters is water depth. **Buoys** often mark shallow areas or rocks where you could damage your center-board or rudder.

Sailing in a Confined Area

Often your boat must be launched in a crowded harbor or anchorage with other boats and shallow water preventing you from just setting forth in any direction. Take a moment before setting sail to survey this situation. Consider the *wind direction and its relationship to the simplest and safest course* out to open water. You should be especially wary of put-

ting the boat into a situation where you cannot turn downwind because of some obstruction. Try to plan your course so that you have *plenty of open water downwind* or leeward of your intended tack. Then if you lose speed from a slow tack or have a problem with the boat, you have room to bear away or drift without hitting anything. When the wind is blowing from the water to the land,

the shoreline is referred to as a "lee shore", and can pose a threat to drifting or disabled boats. This concept of a **"lee shore"** is an important one for all sailors. Again, it all relates to the wind direction, which should always be foremost in your mind when planning your moves in tight quarters.

Another important consideration is your **boat speed**. Remember, as in a car, *with speed comes maneuverability*. Therefore, it is very important to keep your boat moving in tight quarters. Try to avoid excessive tacking or sailing too close to the wind because they both rob speed from your boat.

Some basic right of way rules pertaining to your confrontations with other boats will also come in useful in these tight quarters.

Steering and Sailing Rules

SAME TACK

A book entitled <u>Navigation Rules, International and Inland</u> is published by the U.S. Government with the cooperation of the U.S. Coast Guard. These "Nav Rules", among other things, tell us how boats should steer to avoid a possible collision. In general, when two boats approach one another one of the boats, referred to as the **"Give-way"** boat, must "keep out of the way" of the other boat, as far

as possible, and take early and substantial action to keep well clear. The other boat, referred to as the **"Stand-on"** boat, shall keep her "course and speed" except if the give-way boat does not take appropriate action. These rules should not be confused with racing rules used only by boats sailing in a regatta or yacht race.

An important rule states that sailboats keep their course and

OPPOSITE TACK

OVERTAKING

speed (stand-on) and small powerboats are to keep out of their way (give-way) in order to avoid collision. If possible, a give-way boat should always steer a course that will pass behind the stand-on boat.

There are three basic rules governing sailboats approaching each other. For boats sailing converging courses on opposite tacks, the starboard tack boat is the stand-on boat and the port tack sailboat has to give-way. With sailboats on the same tack the windward most boat should keep clear (give-way). Finally, if you are overtaking another boat on the same heading you must keep clear. Again, if you are charged by the rules to keep clear (give-way) make very clear your intentions to do so. Don't "hot dog" or cut things too closely.

Docking/Mooring/Beaching

Just like sailing in tight quarters the key to docking a boat is *planning and control*. Let us first consider landing your boat at a buoy or dock. Always make your final approach from the *leeward side, sailing on a close reach*. On this point of sail you can really control your speed well without sacrificing too much maneuverability. Do some practice trials in open water near a reference point such as a buoy.

Practice steering the boat on a close reach as you let your sails out by easing their respective sheets. Your speed will slowly drop, but at any time you can trim in the sheets again to accelerate. This technique will allow you to inch up to the dock or mooring buoy under full control. In stronger winds you will have to allow for quite a bit of sideslip (leeway) downwind as your boat slows down.

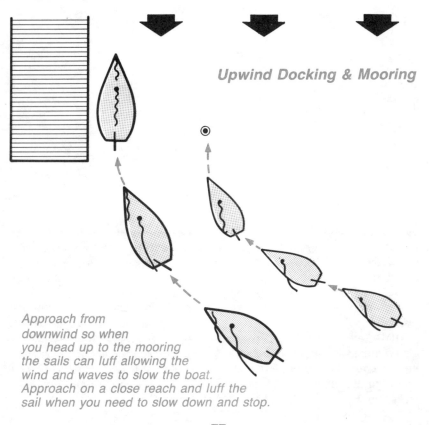

Upwind Docking & Mooring

Approach from downwind so when you head up to the mooring the sails can luff allowing the wind and waves to slow the boat. Approach on a close reach and luff the sail when you need to slow down and stop.

Whenever possible, avoid landing your boat on a dock or beach that requires approaching from windward. This type of landing (known as a *downwind landing*) is extremely hard on the boat and can be quite dangerous because there is no way to slow down. Do whatever you can to avoid a downwind landing, including asking people to move their boats to make space for you on the proper (leeward) side of the dock.

Sometimes a downwind landing is impossible to avoid. This often is the case when landing on a beach that doesn't have multiple sides like a dock. In this case, you will be approaching on a broad reach or run and as you get close you will lift the centerboard halfway (no more or the boat will not turn) so it will not hit bottom. When you are close enough to shore to stand in the water turn the boat into the wind

Downwind Docking

1. Lower jib and secure on deck or stow out of the way.

2. Drop main quickly (don't forget to catch the boom) and coast to a stop at the dock.

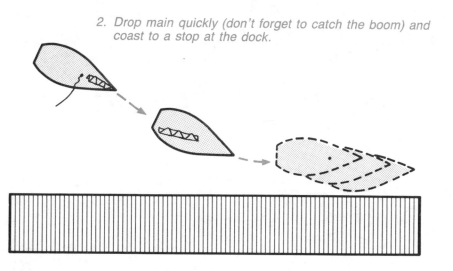

and have a crew member or bystander grab the bow of the boat to keep it pointed into the wind while you lower sails and pull up the centerboard and rudder.

You may occasionally see some hot-dog sailing his boat straight on to a sandy beach. This is really hard on the boat as it is dragged along the sand. If possible have a few people help carry your boat out of the water and gently set it down on sand, padding, or your trailer. Your boat will thank you for it. Practice these skills and learn how your boat reacts to different conditions so you can leave and return to a dock or float safely. If it looks like the docking will not go well, steer away and try again.

Beaching (Onshore Wind)

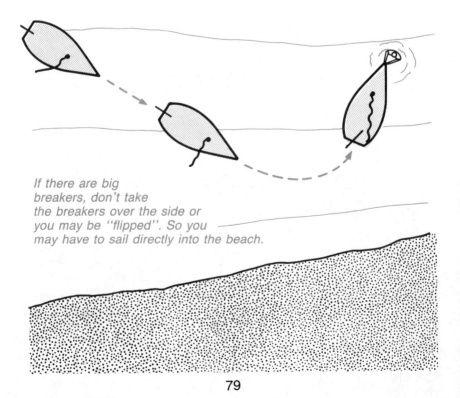

If there are big breakers, don't take the breakers over the side or you may be "flipped". So you may have to sail directly into the beach.

Knots & Line

Though knots are listed last they are a very important part of good seamanship (the art and skill of handling, working, and navigating a ship). Your instructor will explain how to tie these knots easily and quickly. Practice is the "key".

Two characteristics of a good knot are:
- *It holds well (does not come untied)*
- *It is easy to untie even after heavy loading*

These are four helpful knots that sailors use regularly:

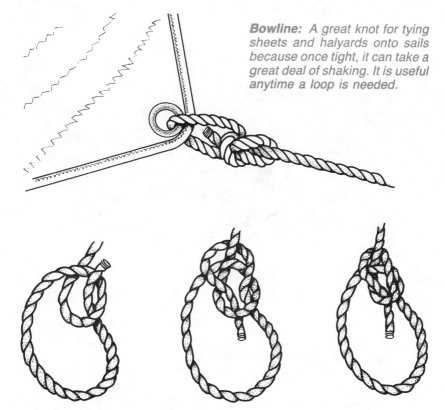

Bowline: *A great knot for tying sheets and halyards onto sails because once tight, it can take a great deal of shaking. It is useful anytime a loop is needed.*

A   B   C

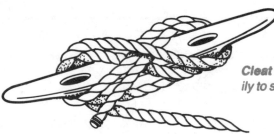

Cleat Hitch: *A knot used primarily to secure the boat to the dock.*

Round Turn and Two Half Hitches: *A good strong knot that is easy to tie. Especially useful in tying the boat to the dock.*

Figure Eight Knot: *A stopper knot to tie in the very ends of halyards and sheets to prevent them from running all the way through a padeye or block.*

Line

There are a number of different kinds of rope or "line" as it's called on a boat. The two most common are dacron and nylon.

Dacron line is known for its "low stretch", that is, its ability not to stretch under load. It's used for sheets, halyards and other control lines and provides accurate sail control under changing loads.

Nylon line is known for its strength and "elasticity", that is, its ability to stretch under load and thus absorb shock or sudden loads. It's used for dock lines and tow lines. Polypropolene line is one kind of line that floats (dacron and nylon line sink) and is used for tow lines and "painters", permanent bow lines on small boats.

81

Review Questions

1. Answer the following statements True or False

a) The crew's side to side position in the boat is a very important way of controlling heel   T   F

b) The rules for trimming a jib on a reach are different than for trimming a mainsail   T   F

c) A good way to determine which jib sheet to trim is to see which side the jib will flap on if all sheets are loose   T   F

d) A centerboard is only necessary in strong winds   T   F

e) Sailors in centerboard boats should be familiar with the underwater topography (rocks and sandbars) that are shown on a nautical chart   T   F

f) Sailors in centerboard boats do not care about the current because it does not affect them

2. When sailing in a confined area...(choose all the answers that are best)

a) Sail very slowly

b) Keep a good lookout, especially in the blind spot behind the sails

c) Keep your speed up because the boat is most maneuverable at top speed

d) Always be aware of the wind direction and the danger of too little open water to leeward of your course (lee shore)

e) You don't have to worry about power boats because you have right of way

3. The best point of sail to approach a dock or buoy at is ...

a) Straight upwind   T   F

b) A close reach because you have the best control over your speed on this point of sail

c) A beam reach because all of your options are open

d) A broad reach because that is the fastest point of sail

e) With all sails lowered, slowly drifting toward the dock

ANSWERS TO REVIEW QUESTIONS

CHAPTER 1	CHAPTER 2	CHAPTER 3	CHAPTER 4
1. d	1. d	1. F,T,F,F,F,T,F	1. T,F,T,F,F
2. a,c,d,e	2. b,c,d	2. a,b,e	2. b,c,d
3. a	3. F,T,F,T,F,F		3. b
4. d	4. a		
5. b			

Glossary

Athwartships: Sailing term for sideways

Beam Reach: Point of sail when the angle between the wind and the boat's course is around 90 degrees

Bearing Away: See heading down

Beating: See close hauled

Boom Vang: Rope pulley system used to hold the boom down to create an efficient sail shape on a reach or run

Broad Reach: Point of sail when the angle between the wind and the boat's course is around 95° – 170°

By The Lee: Dangerous point of sail past running when wind is coming over the same side of the boat as the boom

Capsize: Turning the boat over in the water

Close Hauled: Point of sail when the angle between the wind and the boat's course is around 45 degrees

Close Reach: Point of sail when the angle between the wind and the boat's course is around 85° – 50°

Coming About (Tacking): Changing tacks by turning the bow of the boat through the wind

Current: The movement of water caused by tides or wind

Death Roll: An exciting way to capsize when the boat rolls over pointed straight down

Drysuit: Special sailing or diving suit with special seals that keep person totally dry even when swimming

Feathering: Heavy air steering technique used to reduce heel by steering slightly closer to the wind in order to spill power from the sails

Foulweather Gear: Waterproof outer clothing worn by sailors to stay dry from spray

Groove: Narrow band of steering for efficient close hauled sailing

Halyard: Rope or wire used to hoist sails on masts or on wire stays

Heading Down: Turning the boat away from the wind without changing tacks

Heading Up: Turning the boat towards the wind without changing tacks

Heel: The tilting of the boat caused by strong winds

Hiking Out: Leaning out over the side of the boat to reduce heel

In Irons: Dilemma when boat is "stuck" pointed directly towards the wind with sails flapping and the boat not moving through the water

Jib Halyard: Halyard for the jib, see **Halyard**

Jibing: Changing tacks by turning the boat away from the wind

Jib Sheets: Adjustment rope for the jib; see **Sheet**

Keel Boats: Sailboats that have heavy lead or iron keels that cannot be moved like a centerboard. Usually seen on larger (over 20 feet) boats

Lee Shore: Downwind shore that your boat would blow towards if you were not sailing.

Leeward: Away from wind or downwind side of an object

Life Jackets: Flotation jackets worn by sailors for safety

Luffing: The shaking of a sail like a flag when it is allowed to flow with the wind

Main Halyard: Halyard for the mainsail, see **Halyard**

Main Sheet: Adjustment rope for the mainsail, see **Sheet**

No Sail Zone: An area about 90 degrees wide where a sailboat cannot sail directly because it is too close to the wind direction

PFD: Personal Flotation Device, see **Life Jacket**

Pinching: Same as Feathering

Planing: Sailing along super fast, skimming along over the water on a reach or a run

Points of Sail: Words used to describe the angle between the wind and the sailboat's course

Port: Left side of the boat when facing forward

Port Tack: Words used to describe the boat when the wind is blowing over the boat's left side and the boom is on the right side

Quick Tow: A good way to bail out a swamped "swamper" with a powerboat tow

Reaching: Any point of sail between a run and close hauled

Run: Point of sail when the wind is directly behind the boat

Sea Breeze: Common fairweather, summertime wind on big lakes and oceans. It blows towards the land

Sheets: Ropes used to control the adjustment or trim of a sail (eg., mainsheet, jibsheet)

Starboard: Right side of the boat when facing forward

Starboard Tack: Words used to describe the boat when the wind is blowing over the boat's right side and the boom is on the left side

Swamper: A boat that has no flotation tanks and requires outside assistance to rescue after a capsize

Tacking: See coming about

Telltales: Yarn, sailcloth or cassette tape strands used to show wind direction on shrouds and as an aid in upwind steering on the front of the jib or mainsail

Trapeze: A hiking system used on some boats to allow a crew to stand way out on the edge of the boat, supported by a wire from the mast

Turtling: The position of the capsized boat when the mast is pointed straight down

Wetsuit: Rubber/Neoprene and cloth suit that keeps a sailor warm even if he goes swimming by using body heat to warm the trapped water inside

White Caps: Waves with white frothy tops that are formed in winds over 12 knots

Windward: Towards the wind or side of an object upon which the wind blows

Winging the Jib: Holding the jib out to catch wind on the windward side of the boat. This can only be achieved when sailing on a run with the wind straight behind

Index

Congratulations on your decision to enter the wonderful sport of sailing. We at **Hobie Cat** know you'll discover all the fun, excitement, and pleasure that so many others have already found. As one of the sponsors of this program, we are confident that you have chosen an excellent way to learn sailing skills.

Thousands of sailors around the world have discovered how much fun—and how easy—sailing can be aboard a Holder. Whether it's the **Holder Hawk**, the **Holder 12** or the **Holder 14**, sailors enjoy the performance, value, and quality manufacturing **Hobie Cat** products have always represented.

For more information, write
Hobie Cat
Holder A.S.A. Program
P.O. Box 1008
Oceanside, CA 92054.

ADDITIONAL PUBLICATIONS TO HELP YOU

The following publications are available to you as part of the ASA's program to develop safe and competent sailors. These materials are the Official ASA Texts prepared to help you learn and also meet the Standards leading to *Certification* of your sailing proficiency. Each author was selected for his nationally and internationally recognized expertise in sail education.

Basic Sailing and Basic Coastal Cruising Standards:

Sailing Fundamentals – written by Gary Jobson. 206 pages with two color step-by-step illustrations using over 150 line drawings and photographs. $12.95

Sailing Fundamentals Video Cassette – with Peter Isler. A one-hour fast moving, easy to follow introduction to sailing in four parts which compliments the Text above. Tape is edited by Graham Hall, former U.S. Naval Academy Sailing Coach. Reviewed by *SAIL MAGAZINE* as "one of the best beginning learn-to-sail videos." Includes above Text $49.95

Bareboat Chartering – Intermediate Coastal Cruising Standard:

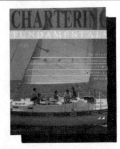

Chartering Fundamentals – written by Brian Fagan. 130 pages with some 60 graphic illustrations and 125 photographs, all well coordinated with the author's comments in providing you the knowledge to cruise or charter with ease and confidence $14.95

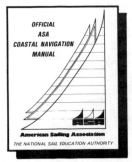

Coastal Navigation Standard:

Coastal Navigation Manual – written by Mike Pyzell. 216 pages in custom looseleaf binder. Well organized and easy to follow, the *Manual* is designed to be used as a self-study course with review questions, answers, and training chart. $59.95

Advanced Coastal Cruising Standard:

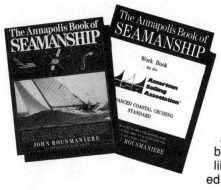

The Annapolis Book of Seamanship – written by John Rousmaniere. 347 pages in two color with more than 700 illustrations and photographs. The definitive guide to sailing based on the principles and curriculum used in the sailing program of the U.S. Naval Academy. An important reference book for your permanent nautical library. Includes Workbook described below $24.95

The Annapolis Book of Seamanship Workbook – written by the same author especially to help you master the broad spectrum of topics covered in the Text $7.95

OTHER ITEMS OF INTEREST

Official ASA Sailing Log Book – 50 page compact format designed to document sailing time; especially useful in qualifying for the Presidential Sailing Award. Also contains International Standards of sailing proficiency and provisions to become certified to those Standards. $6.95

Presidential Sports Award for Sailing – contains all items referenced on inside front cover $6.00

Special 12 month Personal Membership in the ASA – provides benefits including discounts on publications, equipment, services and travel $8.00

"Presidential Sports Award Package" - See description on inside back cover $10.00

Prices subject to change without notice.

ASA ORDER FORM

By special arrangement these prices include shipping and handling. Allow three weeks for delivery. Earlier delivery, including next day, can be arranged for an extra charge. Phone orders are also accepted. You may photo copy this form to place additional orders—a separate form is required for each membership ordered. Thank you for your order and we hope you enjoy the items you have selected . . . .

Please send me the following items:

QUANTITY

TOTAL COST

_____ (M 101P) ASA *"Presidential Membership Package"* @ $10.00 each = $ _____
(Log Book, Certificate, Letter, Patch, 12 month ASA membership)

_____ (L 101) ASA Official *Sailing Log Book* @ $6.95 each = $ _____

_____ (PSA 100) Presidential Sports Award for Sailing @ $6.00 each = $ _____

_____ (M 100) Special 12 month personal ASA Membership @ $8.00 each = $ _____

_____ (L 103) *Sailing Fundamentals* by Gary Jobson @ $12.95 each = $ _____

_____ (VT 100P) *Sailing Fundamentals Video Cassette* with Peter Isler including Text *Sailing Fundamentals* @ $49.95 each =
(Specify: _____ VHS _____ BETA) $ _____

_____ (L 104) *Chartering Fundamentals* by Brian Fagan @ $14.95 = $ _____

_____ (L 105) *Coastal Navigation Manual* by Mike Pyzell @ $59.95 each = $ _____

_____ (L 106P) *The Annapolis Book of Seamanship* by John Rousmaniere including Workbook @ 24.95 = $ _____

_____ (L 107) *The Annapolis Book of Seamanship Workbook* @ $7.95 = $ _____

Prices subject to change without notice.   Total Cost of items ordered: $ _____

Send the above item(s) to: *Please print clearly to avoid error in processing*

Name _____ / _____ / _____
First   Initials   Last

UPS Address **(no P.O. Boxes)** _____
Street

_____ / _____ / _____
City   State   Zip Code

Phone number: Daytime ( ) _____ Evening ( ) _____

☐Enclosed is my _____ check _____ money order in the amount of $ _____

☐You are hereby authorized to charge my credit card in the amount of $ _____

☐American Express   ☐Master Card   ☐Visa

| | | | | | | | | | | | | | | | | | | |
your card number—all digits please   expiration date

Name on the card _____

Signature of Authorized Buyer _____ Date _____

Detach and Mail to:
American Sailing Association
13922 Marquesas Way
Marina Del Rey, California 90292
Phone (213) 822-7171